TEN DORSET MYSTERIES

TEN DORSET
Mysteries

Roger Guttridge

Ensign
PUBLICATIONS

First published in Great Britain by Ensign Publications
2 Redcar Street
Southampton SO1 5LL

Copyright © Roger Guttridge 1989
Reprinted 1990 and 1991

ISBN 1 85455 012 8

Publisher : David Graves
Editorial : Roy Gasson Associates
Typesetting : Robert Harrison
Cover Design : Mark Smith
Printer : Printer Portuguesa

British Library Cataloguing in Publication Data
Guttridge, Roger, 1950—
Ten Dorset Mysteries
1. Dorset. Mysteries
I. Title
001.9'4'094233

CONTENTS

ABOUT THE AUTHOR

Roger Guttridge, born in 1950, was brought up in Dorset and educated at Blandford Grammar School before beginning a career in local journalism. After five years with the *Western Gazette*, he joined the *Evening Echo*, Bournemouth, for whom he has worked successively as Wimborne reporter, chief reporter, deputy news editor, and deputy production editor. He lives at Wimborne with his wife, Sylvie and son, Andrew.

He is the author of two other books on local history, *Dorset Smugglers* and *Dorset Murders*, and was also the editor and joint publisher of Ernest J. Brett's account of a Victorian boating holiday, *Six Men on the Stour*. He is currently writing *Hampshire Murders* for Ensign Publications.

1
Murder in the High Street
The mystery of a Poole double killing, 1598

The ghost of Agnes Beard at Poole's medieval Scaplen's Court is in good company, it seems, for the harbour community is, according to the President of the Ghost Club, Peter Underwood, the most haunted town in Dorset. Agnes's spectral companions in the town centre include an unhappy clerk at the Guildhall Museum, who is said to have hanged himself in the 19th century; a piano-playing phantom and a pair of panic-stricken children at the Crown Hotel in Market Street; a man nicknamed Jenkins, sighted in evening dress on the stairs of a High Street store in the 1960s and 1970s; and a cigar-toting smuggler called Charlie, who was seen at a nearby fashion shop.

Agnes herself is said to appear at Scaplen's Court wearing an apron and to walk from the buttery across the courtyard and up the stairs. Witnesses also talk of a dog heard barking in the historic town house on occasions, even though there is no dog in residence. The apparitions are mysteries in themselves but behind the legend of Agnes Beard's ghost is another mystery of a more earthly kind. It involves the brutal murder of Agnes and her mistress, Alice Greene, almost 400 years ago.

With or without such stories, Scaplen's Court has a colourful past. It dates back to the 15th century and was described by the nation's Chief Inspector of Ancient Monuments in 1950 as "one of the finest examples of a 15th century town house on the south coast". It has been suggested that the eminent antiquary John Leland was referring to it in the 1530s when he visited Poole and described a "fair town house of stone by the Quay". The Poole historian H. P. Smith, who did more than any to ensure the building's preservation in the 1920s, believed it was also the main meeting place of the mayor and his brethren before the Elizabethan Guildhall (since demolished) was built in 1572. Mr Smith also wrote of a tradition, passed on to him in 1924 by Mrs Adey, an eighty-year-old resident of Scaplen's Court, that "royalty once slept in

Photographer Jim Sowerby's interpretation of the Scaplen's Court ghost for the *Bournemouth Evening Echo*.

the building". He speculates that the royal visitor may have been King Henry VII, who visited Poole in 1496. From Mrs Adey, too, he learned of an oil painting that formerly hung over the mantelpiece in her parlour, which bore "the marks of a rapier thrust and a pistol shot".

8

By the 17th century, the building had become the George Inn and probably underwent substantial alteration to make it suitable for its new function. A plethora of initials and dates scratched on the old stone fireplaces suggest that it may also have been used to house troops during the Civil War in the 1640s, when Poole was actively involved in supporting the Parliamentary cause. By the 18th century, it was a dwelling house once again and the home of a Mayor of Poole, Benjamin Skutt, and, later, of the Scaplen family from whom it takes its present name.

Scaplen's Court entered a period of decline towards the end of the 18th century, following the collapse of a stone-mullioned bay window that fronted on to the High Street. As a result, the entire south front was unattractively faced with nine inches of brickwork. The building was eventually converted into eight tenements, which by the early 20th century had deteriorated so much that they were officially condemned as insanitary.

The building's true historic value was discovered by H. P. Smith in the 1920s, when storm damage enabled him to examine sections of the interior. By 1928, the Society of Poole Men, acting at Mr Smith's instigation, had raised enough money to acquire the building, which was restored and opened to the public the following year. Poole Council later took up the cause and today Scaplen's Court is a thriving town-house museum run by the borough museums service.

Whether Scaplen's Court was also the home of Alice Greene and her maidservant Agnes Beard in 1598 is uncertain, but its age, quality, situation, and description are consistent with the information about the building that emerges from the contemporary documents about the double murder case. It was certainly a building fitting to the station in life of Alice's husband, William Greene, a wealthy merchant, who became Mayor of Poole on five occasions and also represented the town as a Member of Parliament.

William Greene, whose assets included a part-ownership of a Poole vessel called the *Mayflower*, died in 1598, leaving most of his £200 estate to his wife—a bequest that did not find favour with his son-in-law, John Beryman, who was openly dissatisfied with his share of the inheritance. Beryman, a merchant and brewer and owner of the Three Mariners Inn, made no secret of his feelings and suggested to Agnes Beard that he ought to receive more.

Agnes was shocked by the suggestion.

"You had your part already," she told him.

"I will have some before I am done!" Beryman replied.

"You shall have no more except you come by it by law!" the

9

Part of the north front of Scaplen's Court in the 1920s showing the 15th century kitchen transformed into tenements.

outspoken maidservant insisted. It was a bold statement for a person in her position to make to an eminent citizen of the town (like his father-in-law, Beryman was a former Mayor of Poole) and Agnes pondered on the long-term consequences.

"I pray to God I may live no longer than my mistress," she confided to a friend.

Her words were to prove tragically prophetic. It was only a few days later that a passer-by heard the sound of barking dogs coming from the High Street house where Mistress Greene and Agnes lived. A light was shining in the hallway but then the dogs suddenly fell silent and the light could be seen moving up the stairs to the first-floor bedrooms. All was quiet and the passer-by continued on his way.

The following morning, there was no sign of life at the house and a boy was sent in through a small window by the stairs to investigate. He was confronted by an appalling scene. In the entrance hall, lying in a pool of blood, was the body of Agnes Beard. She had been struck on the head and stabbed in the temples. In the main hall, also dead, was Alice Greene. Her table was laid for supper and it was clear she had been attacked while eating her meal of buttered pastie. Nearby were the bodies of her two little dogs.

"Murder! Murder!" bawled the horrified youth.

Some of the people outside were too frightened to enter the house, but Nicholas Gibbon, of nearby Thames Street, who was passing when he heard the "cry of murder", called for an iron bar and a sword, intending to charge down the door.

"I ran with the iron bar at the door and found it but closed against me and not locked or barred," he recalled many years later. "I entered the house and found the gentlewoman and her servant there murdered, and many people followed."

An investigation was begun and several people fell under suspicion, including John Beryman, whose conversation with Agnes Beard about her mistress's inheritance was reported by the friend in whom she had confided, Margaret Runnier. Beryman, however, managed to survive the inquiry, which appears to have done his reputation little permanent harm, for he went on to serve a second term as Mayor of Poole in 1602. Instead it was another local man, Roberte Hill, who paid the ultimate penalty, being hanged for the murders in 1599.

The execution of Hill might well have lowered the final curtain on the saga had it not been for the difficulties people had, then as now, in controlling their tongues. In the case of Margery Parmiter, it was anger that caused her to lose control of her tongue. She was the wife of Richard Parmiter, a brewer in the village of Milton Abbas and a former employee of John Beryman at Poole. The marriage was stormy and the couple often quarrelled. During one of these domestic disputes Parmiter called his wife a whore and threw a small hatchet at her.

Margery was incensed. She screamed at her husband: "Murderer! I think thou wilt murder me as thou hast others!"

The episode was witnessed by a servant of the Parmiters, Marie Hill, who was stirring porridge in the kitchen, where the row took place. The year was 1606 and seven or eight years had passed since the killings in Poole High Street but, as tempers cooled, Margery Parmiter realized that, despite the time lapse, she had said too much.

The following morning she summoned the servant girl to her chamber and immediately pushed her behind the door and forced it against her so that Marie was pinned against the wall. Then, waving a knife threateningly under the girl's nose, she swore that she would kill her if she ever dared to repeat the words she had heard the previous day.

Marie Hill (whether or not she was related to the executed Roberte Hill is not known) was able to hold her tongue for almost four years, but on February 25, 1610, Richard Parmiter found himself back in Poole and under arrest. A new investigation was begun and more information began to emerge.

Another who found it difficult to keep anything to herself was Elioner Spencer, wife of another suspect in the 1598 murder case, Gowin Spencer. She could not resist the temptation to tell all she knew to her daughter, Gerrard, and a couple of friends. But she also warned them that if they gossiped in like manner, she would "deny anything she had confessed before".

By the time she was called to give evidence in 1610, she had less reason to be reticent, as her husband had since died. Before the Mayor of Poole, Roger Mawdley, JP, she recalled the evening before the bodies of Alice Greene and Agnes Beard were discovered and the fact that it was 8 p.m. before her husband arrived home for supper. She had prepared a meal of buttered fish, she said, but when she asked Gowin why he was so late, "he answered that I should go to supper for he could eat nothing".

Her testimony continued: "With that I looked on him and found behind in one of his stockings a great black spot and thought it had been a stewed prune. But I put my hand to it and found it did cling to my fingers and proved it to be a clot of thick blood. I demanded of him how he came by it and he answered it was the blood shed of his nose. I then found his cloak was bloody and he did then wash his stocking and his cloak himself and went to bed, eating nothing that night. Later he did dye his cloak black at Wimborne."

The following morning, Elioner Spencer got up early and went outside to fetch some fuel for the fire. When she returned, her husband demanded to know what news she had heard while she was out. She replied that she had heard nothing, upon which Gowin told her that he had brought home 40 shillings the previous night and suggested that she take some of it and go to the market to buy some butter.

"About 11 of the clock," Elioner recalled, "I went again into the market and people reported that Agnes Beard, old Mistress Greene's maid, was murdered. Presently I went home and told Gowin what was reported, to the which he replied, 'So is Mistress Greene killed, too.'"

Elioner could hardly believe what she was hearing. She became distressed and cried out: "You have undone yourself and us all!"

But Gowin Spencer ordered: "Hold thy peace or else, by God, I will knock thy head against the wall!"

Wishing, no doubt, to salvage what she could of her late husband's reputation, the Widow Spencer assured Mr Mawdley that although Gowin was involved in the 1598 incident, it was actually Roberte Hill who committed the murders. She did, however, have a bodkin or small dagger that her husband had brought home after the murders and which she now used as a gardening implement.

"I will fetch him unto Mr Mayor," she said. The "bodkin" was, in fact, a gimlet that Spencer had shaped and sharpened.

Gerrard Spencer, who was only nine when the crimes were committed, grew up to be as much of a gossip as her mother. One witness told how, when the girl was in her early teens, she told several people during a fireside conversation that it was Roberte Hill, Richard Parmiter, and her own father who had murdered the two women. She claimed that before she was killed, Agnes had struggled with her father and had "pulled away a piece of his beard". She also said that, after the murders, the three men went to see John Beryman, who was in bed, and gave him some "writings", which he later burnt, and the bag of money. Her father's cut from the raid amounted to 40 shillings plus some valuable rings and pearls, which he later exchanged at Woodbury Hill Fair, Bere Regis, where he also bought a coat and other things for her.

Several years later, John Beryman was concerned to learn that young Gerrard's tongue was still active. When she arrived at his house one night on an errand for her mother, he called her over to his dinner table and ordered that she "talk no more of his man Parmiter, for that Parmiter was as clear of the murder as himself". Beryman and his wife, Joane, also promised to buy the girl a new petticoat if she kept her silence. She must have done so for a time, for she was later seen wearing a fine new red flannel petticoat beneath her old one, and she explained that it had been given to her by Mistress Beryman but that her mother had told her to wear it underneath where it could not be seen.

13

With the renewed magisterial interest in the murders in 1610, Gerrard Spencer, by now aged about twenty, was presented with the perfect excuse to break her unwritten agreement with the Berymans and tell everything she knew to Mr Mawdley. It was all third-hand information, of course, but the girl was undeterred and when she followed her mother into the witness box she held back nothing.

She told the Mayor that, as she understood it, Parmiter was working for John Beryman at the time and was able to obtain the key to Alice Greene's cellar, which Beryman rented from his mother-in-law. She said Parmiter and his two accomplices, Hill and Spencer, used the key to get into the cellar, which in turn gave them access to a passageway into Mistress Greene's house. They then hid in a small room under the stairs and remained there until Agnes Beard came out of the hall, apparently to fetch some beer from the buttery for her mistress.

"Seeing her in the entrie, Roberte Hill came suddenly on her and struck her on the head with a pressing iron," said Gerrard. "My father then stepped forth and struck into her temples with the bodkin which my mother hath since delivered to Mr Mayor. The three persons went immediately into the hall, where Alice Greene was sitting at supper.

Part of the courtyard of Scaplen's Court in the 1920s.

Roberte Hill took his pressing iron and struck her also on the head. My father and Parmiter in like manner did thrust into the temples of her head with the bodkin. And also they killed the two little dogs by her."

Gerrard said the killers then took the candle from the table and went up into the bedrooms, where they broke open Alice Greene's chests. In one chest they found a bag containing £5, which they divided between them.

"My father had 40 shillings and they also took away divers other things. My father brought his share, two part lots containing a purse of rings and pearls, to our house."

Before the murderous trio left the house, there was one further moment of great tension, for as they reached the entrance hall, they heard a knock on the back door.

"Oh, Lord," Gowin Spencer whispered. "We shall be all taken!"

The men stood in total silence for a time until they were sure that the person at the door had gone. Then they too left, stepping into the dark street outside and closing the door behind them. According to Gerrard, the killers then went to see John Beryman and handed over "certain writings" that they had also stolen.

"He demanded of them what they had done and they answered, 'Murdered Agnes Beard and the old woman,'" said Gerrard. "He replied that he would not have had them to have killed the old woman. After a little while, my father came home with his clothes imbued with blood, and were washed."

Another witness, Marie Gibbon, wife of Nicholas, who was himself now among those under suspicion, spoke of a man rushing out of Mistress Greene's house and almost falling over in his haste as she walked past the building between 7 and 8 o'clock on the night of the murders. Returning a little later, she saw the same man go into either John Beryman's house or the adjoining lane. She added that she understood Beryman's sister-in-law, Cicelie Biggs, was in his house at the time and was frightened by the sudden opening of the kitchen door by a man who then disappeared as quickly as he had arrived.

The testimonies were bad news for John Beryman the brewer and former Mayor who, for the second time in twelve years, was forced to defend himself against the suggestion that he was linked with the double murder. His defence was perfectly straightforward: he flatly denied giving Parmiter the key to the cellar or any other key, denied that Hill, Parmiter, or Spencer visited him on the night of the murders and denied receiving any money or jewellery from his mother-in-law's house.

Parmiter's case was equally uncomplicated.

"On the night of the murder, I was with two fellows and we were brewing in my master's brewhouse, where we continued until 8 of the clock," he said, "at which time we went to our master's house to sup, and after sup to the brewhouse again. We did not go into any house on the way there or back, and remained in the brewhouse until the next day."

Under cross-examination, Parmiter added that while in the street on his way to supper on the fateful night, he "met with certain men and women but their names he knoweth not". In a further outburst, which in the circumstances seems a trifle disloyal to the Berymans, he accused them of using "no speech of sorrow for the murder of Mistress Greene, his master's mother-in-law".

And so the wheels of English justice ground slowly on. What happened next is not entirely clear, but documents relating to the case imply that the Lord Chief Justice visited Poole the following Lent, presumably for the Lent Assizes. What is certain is that John Beryman was acquitted, thanks in no small measure to a change of heart by Gerrard Spencer, who reversed her statement at the crucial time. It was a decision she came to regret, for she found herself shunned by the Berymans and denied sympathy and help by almost everyone else. Soon she wanted to revert to her original claims and in yet another statement, dated July 1611, Gerrard declared that what she told Mr Mawdley the previous year was the truth.

"But I was enforced by my mother," she said, "to forswear and deny it again when my Lord Chief Justice of England did come to Poole in Lent last; or otherwise my mother threatened that she would beat me to death, and that Mr Beryman would hang me if I would not deny it and I would cause Mr Beryman to be hanged. This caused me to forswear and deny that which I knew to be most true. I hope God will forgive me for it, for since the time I and my mother had forsworn ourselves, we never had our health. Now but few pity us or had any remorse of us, to give us any relief as before that they did."

She added, pitifully: "God forgive us for our false oath taken, for it was all true that we had deposed and set down in our examinations at the first."

For John Beryman, life went on as before, and we can imagine that it was all the sweeter following his second escape from the gallows. In her last statement, Gerrard Spencer speaks of him being "brought home bomusey from the fair" after drinking too much, and of those who brought him home being invited to stay for supper. Gerrard, though, was offered "nothing but a piece of bread", while her mother "could have nothing since he was acquitted as before she was wont to have of him".

Exactly what did happen on the night of the murders in 1598 we can only surmise, although it would seem that the hangman did have one of the genuine culprits in his noose when he executed Roberte Hill in 1599. We might also suggest that Gowin Spencer was fortunate to die in his own time. Whether Richard Parmiter was equally fortunate we cannot say, for his eventual fate has not been discovered.

As for John Beryman, we can, again, only speculate about the extent of his involvement. Was he the brains behind the robbery at his mother-in-law's High Street town house? Looking at the evidence that survives, it is hard to detach him from it completely, although it is tempting to think that murder might not have figured in his plans.

Such mysteries and others relating to the case remain, but there is hope that some at least may one day be solved. For although almost four centuries have passed since the Poole High Street murders, the facts that are known have come to light in the relatively recent past and other evidence may yet emerge.

There are, however, a few additional documents that, far from offering solutions to the crime, serve only to heighten the mystery. They date from 1638, four decades after the murders, and were occasioned by the suspicious death of a youth called John Tressler. It occurred at the house of Nicholas Gibbon, who once again came under suspicion and in his testimony referred back to the earlier murders and in particular to the alleged involvement of his old friend Clement Starre. Starre, though in impoverished circumstances at the time, was a talkative fellow and the pair used to enjoy a good gossip about "the business in the town".

"I did delight to have conference with him when in his company," Gibbon admitted. He continued: "Starre told me that there was a great sum of money brought by one Mr Legge of Gissage upon the death of Mr Greene to Mrs Greene's house in Poole, and how safe a matter it was to have the money, for the gentlewoman and her servant were but feeble persons. He dwelt in the next house, where Mr Harwood's kitchen now is, and could see through the tiles of his house where the knitting girls that did work for the gentlewoman and her servant did go forth to supper. He did say it were a safe matter to enter the house and have the money, and I think he did say they might enter through Beryman's cellars but would not swear to it."

Gibbon also recalled that, on the night of the murders, he called at Starre's house to invite him to supper (because he was "a merry pleasant company"), only to be told that his friend was out. On the way home, Gibbon was told about Mistress Greene's barking dogs and the light seen moving up the stairs and the following morning he was

Scaplen's Court before it was reopened as a museum in 1959.

among the first to see the gruesome scene. Later, he said, he was sent for by his neighbour Edward Man, a Justice of the Peace.

"He asked me why my wife had to talk so much about the murder and I told him it was because she thought Clement Starre was a plotter but not an actor," said Gibbon, adding: "This conference was a long time before Hill was hanged, and Clement Starre was found guilty by the Grand Jury. I gave evidence against Starre then, but how he came off I do not remember."

Edward Man's special interest in the case is intriguing, especially as he, like John Beryman, was highly placed in Poole society. So is Gibbon's claim that Clement Starre was found guilty by the Grand Jury. Starre was certainly among the suspects all those years ago but his recollection of events differed from that of Gibbon. Now aged about ninety-three, a grand age indeed in 1638, Starre was called upon to make another statement in which he denied all knowledge of the affair except to admit that he and Beryman were at one stage bound over to appear at the Gaol Delivery in Poole. As far as he could remember, he was released at the first delivery and heard no more about the matter.

2

The Ghost in the Gallery
The mystery of John Daniel's death in 1728

But for the strange events at St Mary's Church, Beaminster, in June 1728, John Daniel would be just another name in the parish burials register. He lived only a short life, of almost fourteen years, and did nothing during those years to set himself apart from the vast majority of his contemporaries. Only the mysterious circumstances of his death and the extraordinary events that followed it cause him to be remembered two-and-a-half centuries later.

John Daniel was descended from a long-established Beaminster family with roots in the area stretching back at least to the 14th century. He was a grandson of James Daniel, an attorney and staunch nonconformist, who fought for the Duke of Monmouth at Sedgemoor in 1685. Despite his advanced years (he is said to have been born about 1611), James survived the battle and returned safely to his home in Hogshill Street, Beaminster. He was, however, pursued by the soldiers of King James II and the emissaries of Judge Jeffreys and escaped only by fleeing across the fields to his farm at Knowle and hiding under straw in a barn. As a tribute to the divine hand that he saw as responsible for his survival, he resolved to be buried on the spot and in 1711, at the age of about 100, became the first of several members of the family to be interred there, in the private burial ground that came to be known as Daniel's Knowle.

John Daniel was born about three years after his grandfather's death and his life was tinged with tragedy from the start. He never knew his mother, Hannah, who died in October 1714, soon after John's birth and just two years after her marriage to his father Isaac Daniel. Isaac remained a widower for less than two-and-a-half years, marrying his servant Elizabeth Stodgell in February 1717 and soon afterwards fathering a second son, Isaac junior. As far as is known, the family lived happily enough for the next ten years. Isaac senior scratched an adequate living from the land—he farmed a smallholding that included thirteen acres of pasture in West Lane and one-and-a-half-acres of arable on Beaminster Down. His sons attended the charity school held daily at the parish church.

But in August 1726 tragedy struck the family again, when Isaac Daniel senior became very sick and died. He was unable to write a will but he conveyed his last wishes orally to the necessary three witnesses and these were recorded in a nuncupative will that was drawn up after his death. In this he left five shillings to each of his two sons and the rest of his goods, chattels, and personal estate to his wife, who was further named as executrix. In accordance with the customs of the Manor of Beaminster Prima, he also exercized his right to nominate whom he wished to succeed to the tenancy of his lands within the manor and so to become the "Lord's next tenant". He chose to nominate his two sons. John was to inherit five acres of pasture and one of arable land; Isaac junior was to have eight acres of pasture and a half acre of arable.

Sadly, John, who had always been a sickly child, enjoyed his tenancy for less than two years. In May 1728, some hours after he was sent out by his stepmother to tend her cows, he was found dead on a small island of sand and gravel formed by the current of a stream about one furlong from his home. According to one contemporary handwritten account, his body occupied a "very odd posture" and there were "several black spots round his neck and on his breast and belly, which tokens of violence". The position of his body, the marks on it, and the "improbability of his voluntarily going to the place where he was found dead" combined to create "great suspicion in the child's relations and neighbourhood that he had been murdered, which occasioned no small stir amongst the people".

There was, however, no firm evidence, and the boy's stepmother allayed people's fears to some extent by disclosing that he had suffered from fits during his lifetime. Thus on Saturday June 1 the body of John Daniel was buried in the churchyard without even an inquest into the cause of death. And that is where the matter would probably have ended were it not for the happenings at the parish church three weeks later, on June 22, 1728.

Exactly what did happen is recorded in two anonymous documents, one the handwritten account that also describes John Daniel's death, the other a letter published in the *Gentleman's Magazine* nearly half-a-century later, in 1774. The two documents are generally consistent with one another but there are enough discrepancies to suggest that they emanated from different sources, which strengthens the case for their authenticity. Both report that the schoolmaster, Mr John Guppy,

The north-west corner of Beaminster church showing the window and blocked up doorway of the gallery which served as a schoolroom.

Photo: Bob Richardson.

who taught his boys in the gallery at St Mary's Church, dismissed the class as usual between 11 a.m. and 12 noon on that June Saturday and that a dozen or so boys lingered in the churchyard to play ball. After a short time, three or four of them returned to the church to clean up and heard a "tingling noise", like the sound of a small bell or a brass pan being struck. The sound seemed to be coming closer and closer, and they ran outside to tell their friends in the churchyard.

At this point the two accounts temporarily diverge in their descriptions of what happened next. The report in the *Gentleman's Magazine* says the boys concluded that there was someone in the church trying to frighten them and they all went back in to investigate but found nothing. "As they were returning to their sport, on the stairs that lead into the churchyard, they heard in the school a second noise, as of a man going in great boots. Terrified at that, they ran round the church, and when at the belfry or west door they heard a third noise, like a minister preaching, which was succeeded by another of a congregation singing psalms; both the last continued but a short time."

The handwritten version makes no mention of the preaching minister or the singing congregation and reports that it was only one of the boys, aged about fourteen, who thought he heard someone coming after him in boots, which caused him to look back as he came down the stairs. "At the farthest end of the school he saw an apparition of a white coffin with brass nails lying on a writing desk there, at the sight of which the said boy cried out and leapt or fell down the stairs in which he bruised himself."

The sources are at one in reporting that the slightly injured boy was quickly joined by the others, four or five of whom stood in the doorway, from where they could see the writing desk. This group then "saw the apparition of the above mentioned John Daniel sitting at a writing desk where he used to write when living". He was in a writing posture and appeared to be wearing his school clothes and hat, which hung over his face. Because of the narrowness of the doorway, only the group of four or five saw the whole apparition, but all the boys were able to see the coffin with its brass nails and a piece of tape or gartering attached to one of its handles.

The first boy to recognize John Daniel was his ten-year-old step-brother Isaac, who is reported to have remarked: "There sits our John, with just such a coat on as I have, with a pen in his hand and a book before him and a coffin by him." The boys went back to their game in the churchyard but returned to the church door from time to time and on each occasion saw the apparition again. Eventually Isaac Daniel, despite advice to the contrary, threw a stone at the figure saying,

"There, Johnny, take it." Instantly the apparition disappeared, leaving the church in a "thick darkness", which lasted two or three minutes.

Word of the boys' supernatural encounter spread quickly, and soon the episode was the talk of Beaminster, adding fuel to the suspicions that had been simmering in people's minds since John Daniel's mysterious death. Some of the dead boy's relatives approached Colonel Brodrepp, JP, of Mapperton Manor, who questioned eight of the boys, aged nine to twelve, individually and was impressed at the extent to which their stories tallied. One of the older boys was regarded as especially reliable, being "sober and sedate" and a newcomer to the school who had never met John Daniel. Despite this, he was able to give an "exact description of the person of the deceased, and took notice of one thing in the apparition which escaped the others, viz. a white cloth or rag which was bound round one of its hands. The woman who laid out the corpse in order to its interment deposed, on oath, that she took such a white cloth from the hand, it being put on it a week or four days before his death, his hand being lame."

One of His Majesty's coroners for Dorset, Mr George Filliter, of Morden, who was also the Town Clerk of Wareham, was sent for and immediately ordered the exhumation of the body. As it was being raised, two of the schoolboys who had witnessed the apparition but had not attended John Daniel's funeral, were heard to remark on the presence of the gartering on the coffin handle as they had seen it in the church.

"The sexton and all others that were present at the boy's burial did not remember that any such string or gartering was left in the handle of the coffin at the time it was laid in the grave," reports the handwritten document.

On July 5, 1728, Mr Filliter sent a message to the parish constables of Beaminster requiring them to warn twenty-four "lawful men of the town and parish" to attend at the King's Arms at 7 a.m. the following day to serve as jurors at an inquest. The written order also named thirty-eight others who would be required to attend the inquest, presumably as witnesses.

The proceedings included the customary viewing of the body by the coroner and jury which, in the middle of summer and following a six-week interment, must have been a dubious experience. A surgeon was present to examine the corpse but was unable to say for certain whether there was any dislocation of the dead boy's neck. The jury were, however, told of the unusual posture of the body when it was found and of the black or blue spots found on the neck. There was further evidence from two women of good repute, who testified that when they saw the body two days after it was found, they noticed a strip of black cloth around the neck. This was confirmed by the joiner who put the boy into the coffin, "for the shroud not being orderly put on the corpse, but cut in two pieces, one laid under and the other over it, gave him an opportunity of observing it". The jury were convinced and returned a verdict that John Daniel died of strangulation.

But was he murdered? Presumably so, but there was little or no evidence enabling the coroner or the jury to point an official finger at anyone in particular. The unofficial fingers of the community at large were less restrained. The author of the handwritten document points out that young John Daniel had been missing for a whole night before his body was found, yet his stepmother failed to instigate any search or inquiries as to his wellbeing or whereabouts. This contributed greatly to people's suspicions, as did a change in her deportment: before the boy's death she was "very gay, singing and merry" and "has since affected to sing but it is observed by the neighbourhood that she pined away. Her lips wale, and in this time in an infirm way." The document even implies that there may have been a motive for Elizabeth Daniel to kill her son, stating that not long before his death, John, "happening to be somewhat infirm, whither by the importunity or love or fear of his mother-in-law (stepmother), or what other motive prevailed on him is not known, but he nominated his said mother-in-law to be the Lord's next tenant to said estate after him". The same document estimates the value of the estate at £300.

Rumours may have been rife but there is no evidence to suggest that Elizabeth Daniel or any other suspect was ever charged or tried for the murder of young John, the exact circumstances of whose death remain a mystery to this day.

The explanation and significance of the apparition in St Mary's church also elude us and are all the more intriguing in the light of a similar incident, which happened six weeks after the first. Like the first, it occurred at the church, though this time on a Wednesday during a weekly service attended by the more devout people of the parish. They included a girl of fourteen—"of very good repute for veracity"—who was kneeling behind her master in the gallery when she suddenly saw a woman push open the door adjoining the stairs and look up at the school area. The young girl touched her master on the shoulder and told him there was a woman at the church door wishing to speak with him. The master, who had a sick child at home, feared that someone had come to tell him the child's condition had worsened and rushed down the stairs, only to see the door slam before him. He went outside but there was no one to be found. He searched "behind

24

The 100-foot tower of St Mary's Church, Beaminster.

Photo: Bob Richardson.

the buttresses of the church wall and corners and all about but could see nobody, which increased his surprise for that it was impossible for any human creature to get out of the churchyard in so short a time".

The noise of the door closing violently had been heard by the minister and the entire congregation and all were mystified, as there was no wind and no person present in a position to open or close it. The girl described the woman as being thin of stature, "rosier with the pox", and with a pale countenance. She was wearing a "sad" or dark-coloured gown, a flowered handkerchief at her neck, and a straw hat on her head. Those who heard the description immediately concluded that the figure must have been the ghost of Hannah Daniel, John's mother, for the description of her person and clothing amounted to a perfect description of her appearance at the time of her death in 1714.

"And it is to be observed," adds the handwritten document, "that the girl who saw her could not possibly describe her, being born about the time of her death."

3

The Gypsies' Alibi

The mystery of the Canning trials, 1753-4

Though they could not have known it at the time, the footsteps trodden by three members of the Squires gypsy family during the last days of 1752 and the opening weeks of 1753 were crucial to their very future. They would be the subject of much debate in a London courtroom and for old Mary Squires would literally mean the difference between life and death. Though seventy years old and somewhat stooped, she was nevertheless a strong and energetic woman. Tall and swarthy, possessing a grotesque lower lip "as big almost as a little child's arm" and a face scarred by the purple marks of scrofula or the King's Evil, she was noticeable enough to leave an impression in the mind of any observer as she trudged through the lanes and by-ways of mid-18th-century Dorset. She said of herself, "If you have once seen my face before, you must have remembered it, for God Almighty never made such another."

On the evening of Friday December 29, 1752, Mary Squires and her son and daughter interrupted their travels at South Perrot, Dorset, staying the night at the Red Lion Inn. They left the following morning and headed for Litton Cheney and Abbotsbury.

"I lay at Litton on the Saturday and left my sister and mother there on the Sunday morning and went to Abbotsbury," said George Squires, the son, giving evidence later. "Mr Clarke had then a good regard for my sister Lucy; he was a sweetheart of her's and she of his. I went to him at Abbotsbury and lay at Gibbons' house one night; then in the morning, which was on a Monday the 1st of January, Clarke and I went to Litton; there we dined upon two fowls which I bought. My mother was surprised at my staying all night at Abbotsbury and she went in pretence to see what was the matter with me, thinking I was sick. There she heard I was gone with Clarke to Litton and she came back again to Litton before we had dined. It is three or four miles. After dinner my mother, sister, Clarke and I walked to Abbotsbury and we danced there that night in Mr Gibbons' parlour. He keeps the sign of the Ship. There were a great many of my acquaintances; I can't tell them all to mind; there was Mr Wallace, a shopkeeper, and Mr Bond, a schoolmaster; he got fuddled that night; Mr Wallace generally drinks cider, he came in for a penny pot of cider. I danced with Gibbons' sister and Mr Clarke with my sister Lucy; we danced country dances till about 11 or 12 at night. We danced several nights there after the first."

The family remained at Abbotsbury for more than a week, leaving on January 9 and being accompanied as far as Portesham, where they slept at the Chequer, and Ridgeway by Lucy's sweetheart, William Clarke. "My mother, sister and I went from Ridgeway to Dorchester on Thursday the 11th, which is about three miles' distance. We did not lie there but went forward almost all night for we had received a letter from my sister Mary, who was at London, that she was extremely ill and desired us to come home as soon as possible. There was a very great water out at Dorchester and the miller's man carried my sister Lucy over it on horseback behind him, for which I told him I'd give him a pint of beer; and I took my mother and carried her on my back through the water. There is a mill just by the place. My sister stayed till we came to her, then we all three walked on together."

From Dorchester they headed for Salisbury, calling at Thorney Down and spending one night at an alehouse at Chettle, another in a barn at Martin, and a third at the widow Greville's house at Coombe Bisset. Their journey to London also took them through Basingstoke, where the literate landlady of the Spread Eagle wrote a letter for Lucy to William Clarke, and through Bagshot, Brentford, and Tottenham. Eventually fate led them to accommodation at Susannah Wells' house at Enfield Wash, north of London. George explained: "We went to a woman's house who sells pease soup at Edmonton. We would have lodged there but my mother wanted to wash and the woman said that was not customary so she recommended us farther to a place called Cheshunt. Upon that we went to Mrs Wells' house being recommended there by Mrs Long's daughter. I left my mother and two sisters at Mrs Wells's house and went to London to receive my money about two or three days after we got there. I lay in London one night and came back the next day."

While George Squires and William Clarke were dining on fowls at Litton Cheney on January 1, 1753, more than 100 miles away a London servant girl was beginning her first day off for ten weeks. That was as long as eighteen-year-old Elizabeth Canning had spent in the employ of the ageing Edward Lyon of Aldermanbury, carpenter to the

Goldsmith's Hall for sixteen years and the former employer of her late father. The post was proving a more acceptable one than Elizabeth's previous job at the Weaver's Arms which, it was said, she had left because the behaviour of some of those who frequented the premises was offensive to her modesty. She was indeed a shy and introverted young woman, prone to fits since a ceiling had collapsed on her when she was fourteen. But she was a good worker and the Lyons were as pleased with her as she was with them. When Christmas came, Mrs Lyon decided to reward Betty Canning with a present of half-a-guinea in gold and three shillings in silver. She also promised her a holiday on New Year's Day.

When the day arrived, Elizabeth dressed herself in her best clothes, which included a bright gown of purple shot with yellow, a black quilted petticoat, and a white hat with green ribbons. Beneath she wore stays—worth ten shillings—and a coarse linen shift, patched in places. Some time before noon, she set off to walk to her widowed mother's house at Aldermanbury Postern, taking with her, concealed in a petticoat pocket, her Christmas box of gold and silver coins.

She left her mother's to dine with her aunt and uncle, Thomas and Alice Colley, in Saltpetre Bank. There, she found herself eating the leftovers of the previous day's meal, namely cold shoulder of mutton and cold potatoes. Aunt Alice promised to make up for this by providing a hot supper if her niece would stay until the evening. Elizabeth accepted and whiled away the afternoon watching her uncle pursue his trade of glass-blowing. For tea she was served buttered toast and for supper roast sirloin of beef, but it was noted that in both cases she did little more than nibble at the food.

The Lyon family expected Elizabeth to return by 9 o'clock that evening, but it was already that when she set out. Her aunt and uncle accompanied her to Houndsditch, almost as far as the Blue Ball, and watched as she disappeared into the darkness. By this time Edward Lyon was already on Mrs Canning's doorstep, intending to reprimand her daughter for not returning on time. Elizabeth, of course, was not there. An hour later her employer was back again; Elizabeth had still not returned.

"I was frightened out of my wits," Mrs Canning recalled later. "I sent my three children into the fields to see after her and I sent my apprentice to Mr Colley's, her uncle; they said they had parted with her after nine o'clock at Houndsditch. I sent again in the morning and I went myself before it was light. Mrs Colley was a'bed then. I said: 'Let me in, let me in.' Mrs Colley got up and said: 'O lack, has not she come in yet?' I said: 'No.' She said she left her there. Her husband was called from the glass-house; and I was ready to run distracted."

Mrs Canning began to scour the neighbourhood in search of her daughter. She knocked up her neighbours, waking those who were still in bed; she trudged anxiously and wearily from hospital to hospital. Uncle Thomas Colley joined in, taking two young helpers on a tour of watch-houses and pubs, but no one had seen the girl in the purple and yellow gown.

The family decided to try a different approach. Using a quill and a sheet of paper, Aunt Alice wrote out the words of a public notice as dictated by the tearful Mrs Canning: "Lost, a girl about eighteen years of age dressed in a purple masquerade stuff gown, a white handkerchief and apron, a black quilted petticoat, a green under coat, black shoes, blue stockings, a white shaving hat with green ribbons, and had a very fresh colour. She was left on Monday last near Houndsditch, and has not been heard of since: whoever informs Mrs Canning, a sawyer, at Aldermanbury Postern, concerning her, shall be handsomely rewarded for their trouble."

The notice found its way to the coffee houses of London through the columns of the *Daily Advertiser* but Mrs Canning waited in vain for a positive response. Friends had a whip-round to pay for a second advertisement: "Elizabeth Canning went from her friends between nine and ten on Monday night, betwixt Houndsditch and Bishopsgate, fresh-colour'd, pitted with the smallpox, high forehead, light eyebrows, about five foot high, well-set, had on a purple masquerade-stuff gown, black stuff petticoat, a white chip hat bound round with green, white apron and handkerchief, blue stockings, and leather shoes."

Before the document was completed, it was learned that a shopkeeper in busy Bishopsgate Street had heard a young person screaming from a coach as it was hastily driven off. At the time she thought it was a boy's voice but it could have been a girl's. The news prompted Tom Colley to put up a two-guinea reward and a postscript was added to the notice: "Note, it is supposed she was forcibly taken away by some evil-disposed person, as she was heard to screek out in a hackney coach in Bishopsgate-street. If the coachman remembers anything of the affair, he shall be handsomely rewarded for his trouble."

The second advertisement produced no response. The days turned into weeks. Mrs Canning spent much of her time praying and much of the remainder asking others to do the same. She even consulted a conjuror or clairvoyant. For a shilling, he told her that her daughter was in the hands of an old woman and would return shortly; he also advised her to publish a third advertisement, which she did.

At 10.15 p.m. on Monday January 29, Mrs Canning knelt at her bedside to pray as usual. She had urged her apprentice sawyer, James Lord, to follow suit, but first he had to perform his nightly duty of locking up the house. He was about to do so when they both heard the latch lift.

"Here is somebody at the door," said Lord as it slowly opened.

"Who is it?" Mrs Canning inquired.

Lord could scarcely believe his eyes as Elizabeth Canning staggered in, bent almost double and swaying from side to side, her hands held before her.

"'Tis Betty," said Lord.

"What Betty?" asked his mistress.

"Our Betty!"

The young woman was in an appalling state and Lord would never forget the sight before him.

"She was," he recalled later, "e'en almost black and blue; she was dressed up with an old bit of an handkerchief round her head and an old dirty ragged bedgown, what they properly call a jacket. She had no cap, nor hat, nor stays on; her ear was cut and all bloody. Her face and hands would compare for blackness to a hat almost; the colour of her flesh was next akin to the colour of beating."

One look at her daughter's face, all swollen and blue, one glance at her emaciated body and the rags that clothed it, caused Mrs Canning to faint. When she recovered, she sent James Lord to fetch help and began to attend to Elizabeth's most immediate needs.

Neighbour Mary Woodward was the first to arrive. She too was shocked by Elizabeth's condition.

"Oh, Mrs Woodward," cried the girl. "You don't know how I have suffered, for I have been almost starved to death. I have had nothing but bread and water since new year's day at night, and I have had no bread ever since Friday."

Explaining that she had been held in a room in a house on the Hertfordshire road, Elizabeth continued: "On new year's night, when I came away from home, my uncle and aunt came with me as far as Houndsditch. From thence I came alone over Moorfields. At Bedlam gate I was met by two men who stopped me. They took my money out of my pocket. . ."

"How much money?" Mrs Woodward interjected.

"Half-a-guinea in gold, in a little box, and three shillings in silver. They dragged me up the fields facing Bedlam. One of the men held me, and the other took away my hat, apron and gown, all which he put

ELIZABETH CANNING
Drawn from the Life.

Elizabeth Canning.

into his greatcoat pocket. Then they tied my hands behind me, and he that held me said: 'Damn you, you bitch, we'll do for you!' Then he struck me on the head, which threw me into a fit directly."

When she emerged from her fit, Elizabeth had found herself in a roadway between the two men. Soon afterwards they met a third man, who asked: "What luck tonight, brother?" to which they answered: "I'll tell you better in the morning." After about half-an-hour, said Elizabeth, they came to a house where she saw an old woman and two young women. The old woman took her by the hand and said that if she would "go their way" she would have fine clothes.

"I answered no," said Elizabeth. "Then the old woman went to a dresser and fetched a knife and cut the lace of my stays and took them from me. The young wenches did nothing but laugh. Then the old woman took up my petticoats and gave me a slap on the face and said: 'Damn you, you bitch, they are good for nothing, I'll give you them.' Then she turned me upstairs, saying if I cried out, she would come and cut my throat."

"What sort of woman was she?" asked Mrs Woodward.

"A tall, black, swarthy woman," Elizabeth replied. She went on: "At daylight, I looked about me and the first thing I took notice of was a black jug. It was broke at the neck and in it was near a gallon of water. Near to it was some pieces of bread, in quantity about a quartern loaf. There was also a basin. On looking further about the room, I saw a grate in the chimney, and therein an old bedgown. I put it on to keep me warm."

"Have you never been in bed?" Mrs Woodward asked.

"I have never been in bed since I lay at my master Lyon's."

Next to arrive behind Mrs Woodward were Polly Lyon and Mary Myers. By this time, Elizabeth Canning was reduced to a sobbing jelly, but she managed to compose herself sufficiently to whisper the tale a second time. She went further and described the manner of her escape.

"I pulled down a couple of boards that were fastened against the window," she said. "I put out my head and shoulders, took hold of the window and drew out my legs, and so dropped down. And that is how I tore my ear. I escaped about four in the afternoon and asked my way to London. While I was in the room, there was a staircase lay close to the room and I heard people run up and down in the nights and I heard the name mentioned of Wills or Wells."

News of Betty Canning's return spread rapidly and soon others began to appear, some summoned by Lord, others uninvited. They included John Wintlebury, landlord of the Weaver's Arms and

Elizabeth's former employer, and Robert Scarratt, who lodged with a neighbour and earned his living by rasping or grating hartshorn for the production of ammonia. Between words of comfort, Wintlebury asked the half-starved girl how she knew the place of her imprisonment was on the Hertfordshire road.

"I remember seeing the Hertford coach when I looked through the chinks in the window," she replied. "It was the coach that used to carry my mistress into Hertfordshire."

"How far were you from London?" asked Wintlebury.

"About ten or eleven miles."

"Do you know the name of the person who kept the house?"

Scarratt, like Wintlebury, knew the Hertford Road. His excitement was growing with every word and it was he and not Elizabeth who answered first.

"I'll lay a guinea to a farthing she has been at Mother Wells', for that is as noted a house as any is," he said.

Someone produced some toast and warmed white wine in which to dip it. Elizabeth was unable to swallow the toast but the wine seemed to revive her.

"I'll be hanged," Scarrat repeated, "if she has not been at Mother Wells' at Enfield Wash. Pray, what like woman was she?"

"A tall, black, swarthy woman. She robbed me of my stays," said Elizabeth.

"This is not Mother Wells. I have seen Mother Wells and to the best of my knowledge that description does not answer her," said Wintlebury. He left the Canning house at this point but Scarratt was nowhere near finished.

"Wells has two daughters. Were there any daughters there?" he inquired.

"There were two young women there, one with black hair and one with fair," said Elizabeth. "They stood laughing at me while my stays were cutting off. But whether they were her daughters or not I could not tell."

Again she described the darkish room in which she was held and the damaged water jug holding four or five quarts.

"The window," said Scarratt. "Did it front the road?"

"No, it was in the back part of the house."

"Did you come into the main road immediately after you got out of the house?"

"No. I turned down a little lane and then turned into the fields on my right hand."

"When you was in them fields, on which hand was the road?"

34

"On the right hand coming to London."

"Do you remember if, in coming out of them fields to the main road, you crossed a footbridge over a little brook close to a house?"

"I did."

"Was it a tanner's house?"

"Yes. Yes, it was," said Elizabeth.

It was all the proof that Scarratt needed. Mother Wells was to blame, for certain. "It was Mr. Neal's, a tanner, at Enfield Wash," he said, triumphantly.

Sharing a room with her mother, two little sisters, and a baby, Elizabeth slept well that night and next morning was visited by an apothecary, to whom she complained of feeling faint and sick, of a pain in her bowels, and of constipation.

Meanwhile, Elizabeth's outraged friends and neighbours were opening their campaign to avenge the dreadful treatment she had suffered and bring the perpetrators to justice. There was no doubt in their minds as to the identity of the main perpetrator. On January 31, a new advertisement appeared in the *Daily Advertiser*. It described Elizabeth's capture and went on: "They then forcibly carried her to Enfield, to a house kept by one Mother Wells, near the Wash, by the ten mile stone, which place they reached about four o'clock in the morning. The fellows left her in that house and she has not seen them since. The woman of the house immediately cut off her stays with her own hands and with the horridest execrations forced her into a room, where she was kept upon bread and water. She broke her way through a window almost naked and in that wretched condition came home. She left several unhappy young women in the house, whose misfortune she has providentially escaped."

At noon the same day, Elizabeth, still barely strong enough to walk, found herself heading for the Guildhall on a coach, flanked by fifty supporters. Once again she told her story, this time to the sitting alderman, Thomas Chitty. Her supporters demanded that a warrant be issued.

"Against whom?" Alderman Chitty asked.

"Against Susannah Wells of Enfield Wash," came the collective reply. Copies of the *Daily Advertiser* were thrust forward to back up the demand.

"How do you come to know that you were at Mother Wells?" Chitty inquired.

"I heard her called so when I was confined in that room," the girl replied.

"Be sure what you say. Say nothing but what you can swear to," warned the alderman.

The warrant was duly issued and later endorsed by a Middlesex JP.

Early the following day, a small army of volunteers set off for Enfield Wash to confront Mother Wells. Edward Lyon and three of his cronies from the Goldsmith's Hall travelled together in a mourning coach; Wintlebury, Scarratt, and leather-dresser Joseph Adamson went on horseback; Tom Colley and baker Edward Rossiter went on foot. For Elizabeth herself and the female section of the entourage, a chaise was provided.

The cavalry arrived first, at 9. a.m., and tethered their horses at the Sun and Punchbowl, strategically placed within sight of Mother Wells' house across the way. While one of the trio kept watch, the others gathered intelligence from landlord John Cantril and a pledge of support from a schoolmaster called Ball. They learned, among other things, that Mother Wells was not at home and that her lodgers included four members of a family called Squires.

By the time Mother Wells had returned, the Lord Mayor's officer, William White, had arrived to join the advance party and, together with Ball and the parish constable, they moved forward purposefully towards the house and through the front door. The head of the house was in the parlour with some of her guests.

"That is she!" bawled Adamson, levelling his finger at her wizened face.

"You are all prisoners!" cried White, drawing his sword. He instigated a search and found old Mrs Squires and her two daughters in one of the bedrooms and ordered them to the parlour.

Mr Ball the schoolmaster found George Squires in another room bundling up his belongings ready for a quick getaway.

"Where are you going?" he asked. "You must not go away."

Squires tried to escape through a window but Ball called for reinforcements and soon the gypsy man joined his family and hostess in the parlour. He demanded to know the reason for his detention.

"There has been a robbery," said White.

"When was the robbery committed?"

"On the 1st of January."

"We were in Dorsetshire at that time," said Squires. "At a place called Abbotsbury. We went there to keep our Christmas."

The gypsy women confirmed his story and Squires invited the party to search his effects. In the event, they searched everyone's and in the process discovered Mother Wells' daughter, Sal Howit, and two other lodgers, Virtue Hall and Judith Natus. But they did not find the stolen stays. Joseph Adamson also looked into the bedrooms but each contained a bed and thus failed to fit Elizabeth's description of her prison, which was dark and almost empty and had no bed. The loft, however, while containing an old chest of drawers among many other things, had a pile of hay as its only bed. There were two windows, one narrow, fronting the stairs, with a glass casement, the other half glass and half boarded up.

In due course, the infantry arrived, and Tom Colley joined Adamson in his investigations. They thought they could see broken plaster beneath the loft window and fresh fragments on the ground below. They showed them to White as evidence that this was the escape window but his eyes were unable to detect the fragments. White was also unable to see any sign of footprints in the soft ground or the pile of human dung beneath the window such as would have been left by an escapee.

By the time Edward Lyon and his Goldsmiths arrived, it was past 11 a.m. They began to interrogate George Squires, who told them he was a travelling pedlar who had come to winter at Enfield Wash instead of his own house at Newington Butts because he had debts and feared the bailiffs. He spoke of an influential relative at Southwark—one Samuel Squires, who was in the Customs—whom he hoped would help to solve his financial problems.

Lyon's friends Gawen Nash and Edward Aldridge took themselves on a tour of the house. Meeting the Lord Mayor's man, Nash inquired: "For God's sake, what do you think of this affair?"

"I think we are got into the wrong box," White replied. "The girl was never in this house."

The girl herself had still not arrived and Adamson was despatched to locate her vehicle and hurry her up. It was his first meeting with the Aldermanbury servant girl since her ordeal.

"Bet," he asked, "what sort of room was you in?"

"Sir," she replied, "it is an odd sort of an empty room, there is hay and a fireplace in it."

Adamson galloped back to Wells' house, waving his hat in the air, and announced excitedly: "By God, we are all right yet, for she says there is a little hay in the room."

It was Adamson, too, who carried the weak and helpless girl into the house when she arrived. She needed mulled wine to revive her, then an identity parade was organized and the girl urged from various quarters to be certain before fixing on anyone. She was taken to the parlour, where Mother Wells and her guests were seated around the fire.

"Why, the girl is sick," sneered Wells, contemptuously. She got to her feet. "Madam," she added, looking straight at Elizabeth. "Do you know me?"

37

"No," said the girl. "I don't know that ever I saw you in my life before."

The visitors were stunned. Then George Squires stepped forward.

"Madam," he demanded. "Do you know me?"

"No," said Elizabeth. "It was that old woman in the corner that cut my stays off."

She pointed at Mary Squires, but it was the old gypsy's daughter Lucy who replied.

"Do you hear what the gentlewoman says? She says you cut off her stays."

Old Mary stirred for the first time and rose to her feet.

"Madam," she said in turn. "Do you say I robbed you?" Pulling back clouts which partially covered her face, she added: "Look, for God's sake. Look at this face. If you have once seen it before, you must have remembered it, for God Almighty, I think, never made such another. I am a very remarkable woman, I have got the evil in my face, and you may know me by night or by day."

The frail girl was unmoved. "I know you very well. I know you too well, to my sorrow," she said.

The gypsy demanded to know when she was supposed to have committed this robbery. It was on the first day of the new year, she was told.

"The first day of the new year, madam, do you say? Lord bless me! I was 120 miles from this place then," protested the older woman. "I was at Abbotsbury in Dorsetshire and there are a hundred people I can bring to prove it. And some of them have known me 20, 30 and 40 years."

Others among the Enfield Wash inhabitants confirmed that the gypsies had been there no more than eight days but Elizabeth was undeterred. She levelled an accusing finger at Lucy Squires and claimed: "This young woman was leaning on the dresser when my stays were cut off." And turning to Virtue Hall, she announced: "And this one was standing by her. But they did nothing to me."

As Virtue Hall protested her innocence, George Squires was ushered forward a second time with the suggestion that he might have been one of the Bishopsgate Street abductors. Elizabeth considered the matter carefully before pronouncing.

"No," she said. "He looks very like one of the men but I will not positively swear to him."

After a further identity parade staged to make doubly sure, Elizabeth was invited to consider the location of her prison. She declared that she believed the staircase to be the one up which she had been taken but she was equally certain that the site of her confinement was not one of the first floor bedrooms. When presented with the second staircase leading to the loft, she declared she had not been carried so high; but once inside she changed her mind.

"Yes," she said, looking around. "This is the room I was confined in."

Elizabeth was invited to examine everything in the room. Someone spotted a black jug with a damaged neck and she identified it as the one she had drunk her water from. She also recognized an instrument used for measuring out tobacco but remembered only one of three saddles in the room, even though all were covered with the dust of ages. Someone asked if she remembered the nest of drawers which had clearly sheltered generations of spiders. She did not. Nor did she recall a pulley hanging from the ceiling, nor a glassless casement sealed to the wall by cobwebs.

"Zounds, child, I cannot think you were ever here at all," said Hague. Holding the girl with one hand, he opened the small glass casement window which fronted the stairs with the other. "How came you, child, not to get out here? You see it is very easy."

"Sir", said Elizabeth, "that was nailed up when I was here. I tried to open it but could not."

Not for the first time, it was Adamson who came to the rescue. Placing himself between the girl and the window to obscure her view, he said: "If you have been confined in this room so long, you will be able to give a very good account of it—and I expect you will."

Elizabeth, standing six feet from the window, answered without hesitation.

"Trees and fields and a hill in the distance," she said. "And to the left a little lane with houses."

The description was impressively accurate. Next Adamson asked Elizabeth where she looked out to see the Hertford coach. She pointed to the end window.

"That is the window and that is also the window I made my escape out at," she said.

On examination it was found that the boards on the window had been freshly nailed up, and probably not by a man. Not everyone was convinced, in particular Edward Lyon's friends from the Goldsmith's Hall, but the evidence was enough to satisfy Adamson and the Aldermanbury contingent. It was time to bring the Enfield villains before a magistrate and preparations began to take them on a cart to the nearest court. There, Mary Squires was committed to New Prison for stealing the stays and Mother Wells to the Bridewell for being a bawd and running a disorderly house.

Though Mary Squires had recently been seen about Enfield, she was little known there, but of Susannah Wells the opposite was true. Her past was a colourful one and few were surprised to learn of her arrest. Her background in harlotry had taken her to prison on at least one previous occasion and she was always prepared to "let lodgings" to couples seeking a bed.

A few days after the arrests of the two older women, Judith Natus and Virtue Hall also found themselves in court, this time at Bow Street before Mr Justice Fielding, otherwise the novelist Henry Fielding. Natus vehemently denied ever seeing Canning in Wells' house, adding throughout the period in question she and her husband had slept in the room of "her pretended confinement." Hall, however, told a very different story. Between sobs, she described the girl's arrival in the house, the conversation between Wells and the two men, one of whom she called John Squires, reputed son of Mary, and the removal of Elizabeth to the workshop at the top of the building. She added that after Elizabeth's escape was discovered, the Natus couple began sleeping in the room instead of the kitchen to give the impression that they had been there all the time, while Wells' daughter Sarah nailed up the escape window so that it might not appear to have been broken open.

Following this testimony, the bawd and the gypsy woman were transferred to Newgate to await their trial and a reward was offered by the men of Aldermanbury for the arrest of George Squires, who had disappeared. Appeals were also made for donations to help finance the prosecution or to be "given to the poor girl as a recompense for her virtue and miseries she had gone through." Her ordeal, and her apparent success in protecting her virtue despite it, had made her a popular heroine.

The trial began at the Old Bailey on February 21. The defendants pleaded not guilty, the gypsy to stealing the stays, Wells to feloniously receiving, harbouring, comforting, concealing, and maintaining their wearer. Elizabeth Canning herself was the first witness and once again she trotted out her terrible tale, standing up well to cross-examination by William Davy, a former Exeter grocer who was now becoming a living legend as a London lawyer. Virtue Hall followed her into the witness box and gave evidence which was both damning to the defendants and a little confused. She claimed the gypsies had been in the house a fortnight when Elizabeth arrived and were there six or seven weeks in all. But her description of the sequence of events did not quite tally with the account she had given to Justice Fielding at the earlier hearing.

After evidence from the remaining prosecution witnesses, including Elizabeth Canning's mother and several of her supporters, the defence pulled out what they believed to be the first of their trump cards.

"I live at Abbotsbury, six miles from Dorchester. I am master of the house called the Old Ship," John Gibbons told the court. "On the 1st of January 1753, the prisoner Squires came into the house; there was George her son and Lucy her daughter with her, as she called them. She came with handkerchiefs, lawns, muslins and checks to sell about town. She stayed there from the 1st to the 9th day of the month and lay at my house."

William Clarke and Thomas Greville gave supporting evidence, the former telling how he walked with the gypsies towards Dorchester on January 10, the latter how he put them up at the Lamb pub at Coombe Bisset, near Salisbury, on January 14. Each of the trio was asked in cross-examination how he remembered the date and each had a convincing answer. Gibbons had a written record of the date because it coincided with the visit of an Excise officer; so did Clarke, because he had noted his delivery of goods to Portesham in his accounts book; while Greville could pin down their visit to a Sunday because he had had cause to turn out a wayward carpenter on account of his behaviour on the holy day.

"Do you remember when you kept Christmas day?" the prosecuting counsel asked of Clarke.

"I do not."

"Can you give any account of new style or old?" The question referred to a recent change in the calendar. To bring the nation in line with Europe's Gregorian calendar and the cycles of the Sun, the Government had decreed that the day after September 2, 1752, would be called September 14, thus dropping 11 days from the calendar and causing an outbreak of national confusion with, for example, some people celebrating Christmas on December 25 and others on January 2. Come 1753, the populace had to cope with the additional complication of two calendars, old-style and new.

"No, I cannot," Clarke replied, adding: "But if I was to die for the woman, I'll speak the truth."

Mary Squires' defence was impressive, though the prosecution called rebuttal evidence from a fish seller who claimed to have seen her "pretending to tell fortunes" in the Waltham Cross area three weeks before her arrest. Mother Wells' case, on the other hand, was hopeless. She had no lawyer and offered no witnesses.

"As to my character," she told the court, "it is but an indifferent one; I had an unfortunate husband who was hanged. But I never saw the

Mary Squires the Gypsy, who stript Eliz.ª Canning, at Enfield Wash. Drawn while She was on her Examination before Justice Fielding, by the Honourable R__ E__ and Etched by Thos Worlidge Painter in the Piazza, Covent Garden.

MARY SQUIRES

Mary Squires the gypsy.

young woman till they came to take us up. And as to Squires, I never saw her above a week and a day before we were taken up."

The jury were unconvinced. To the approval of the majority of spectators, they found both women guilty. Five days later, they were sentenced, Squires to death, Wells to six months in Newgate and instant branding on the thumb. But there were people who had doubts and they included the trial judge, Mr Justice Gundry, who happened to be a Dorset man, and Sir Crisp Gascoyne, the Lord Mayor of London. Both resolved to check out the gypsy woman's alibi.

While Elizabeth Canning was being re-equipped with stays and other garments by the more generous of her many supporters, new evidence was beginning to trickle in. It included letters from the vicar of Abbotsbury, Mr Harris, and the under-sheriff of Dorset, Mr Willis.

"I have this morning," the vicar wrote, "sent for several of my parish who well know this woman and her companions, one particularly with whom they always lodged till last time of their coming here. And he tells me that he has known this Mary Squires upwards of 30 years; that she, with others of that name, and some of other names, have in that space of time often come to this house, sometimes once or twice in a year, at other times once in two or three years; that they (this Mary Squires and others) were at his house about three years ago, which was the last time they were at Abbotsbury till the 1st of January last. That he often saw them at the house of John Gibbons between the 1st and the 9th of January; that they always went under the denomination of gypsies, that they had goods (as handkerchiefs, aprons, gowns, etc.) to sell, that they never wanted money and always paid very justly for what they had. Their being here this last time could be proved by most of the younger sort in my parish, for as it was Christmas-time they had dancing almost every night at the house, and the son and daughter of Squires danced constantly with the people of the town."

Sir Crisp Gascoyne also questioned Virtue Hall who, after long consideration, admitted that the story she gave at the court hearings had been "all false".

"When I was at Mr Fielding's, I at first spoke the truth," she explained. "But I was told that that was not the truth, and they terrified me and threatened to send me to Newgate and prosecute me as a felon unless I would speak the truth, until in the end I swore what was false to save my own life."

The Lord Mayor went to see Wells and Squires at Newgate. Squires had contracted gaol distemper and was too ill to be seen. Wells again strongly denied that Canning was ever in her house or that the gypsies were there more than eight days. Sir Crisp was also visited by a deputation from Enfield Wash, including Wells' son and daughter and Judith Natus and her husband, Fortune, all of whom claimed to be in a position to confirm the innocence of the two convicted women.

Two other visitors to the London Mansion House were blacksmith and fiddler Melchizedeck Arnold and carpenter John Ford, who travelled up from their home village of Abbotsbury to have their say.

"I know the woman well," Arnold told a sizeable audience which included some of Elizabeth's supporters as well as the Lord Mayor and his people. "I saw her and George her son and Lucy her daughter at the Old Ship in Abbotsbury, Gibbons' house, on the 1st day of January last. On that very evening, My Lord, I played on the violin to some young people who were dancing. George and Lucy were of the number and Mary Squires sat by the kitchen fire. And on the 6th of January, being twelfth day in the evening, there was another match of dancing at the Old Ship, and George and Lucy were of that party; and I played to the dancers, and Mary Squires sat by the fire and looked on. And I saw her about Abbotsbury divers other times during that new year's week."

"Do you mean old style or new?" Arnold was asked.

"My Lord, I mean this present calculated time."

"My Lord, this is all true," came in John Ford. "I have known the woman this three years past. John Gibbons is my nephew and I live directly across the way from his inn. I saw these people about town from the 1st to the 9th of January last, and on the 9th, it was a Tuesday, they went away. I sell bread and tobacco, My Lord, and divers other goods, and they used frequently to come and buy things of me during their stay."

Canning's friends could only stand and complain that the Abbotsbury bumpkins were not to be trusted.

"The people of the seacoast are notoriously smugglers and wreckers of ships," said one.

"All of them," said another.

"Not excluding the vicar," muttered a third.

Once the visitors had gone, the Lord Mayor ordered his clerk to write two further documents. One was a letter requesting the presence of the Dorset Excise officer who had stayed at the Old Ship, one Andrew Wake, together with his Excise books. The other was a warrant for perjury against Elizabeth Canning.

Wake arrived at Newgate on March 18, 1753, and then went on to the Mansion House. There, he confirmed that he was sent to Abbotsbury on December 31 to stand in for another exciseman who was sick. He stayed there until January 14 and he had his books to prove it. And he remembered the gypsies well and had even borrowed George Squires' coat to go on his rounds when there was snow and his was wet through.

"Have you seen the convict in Newgate?" the Lord Mayor asked.

"My Lord, I have, and she is the same woman. She was in the press yard, she knew me through the grate and greeted me. I asked her if she knew me. She said yes, that I was the young man belonging to the excise office and she remembered me very well. She seemed rather overjoyed to see me and reminded me that I borrowed her son's greatcoat."

Wake went to see the gypsy in gaol a second time and she reminded him of how, when he came in ill, she had made him a hot potion to cure him; and a day or two later she had made him hot buttered toast before he went out.

"'Twas no later than February 7," he told Canning's friends, "when I read a newspaper to my mother at Dorchester wherein was some account of Mary Squires the gypsy woman being taken up for a robbery, upon which I in great surprise said to my mother : 'This can't be, for this is the woman I saw at Abbotsbury whilst I was there.'"

The evidence supporting the Squires alibi was now flooding rather than trickling in. A midwife who had examined Elizabeth upon her return arrived at the Mansion House to testify that she had been wearing a shift which was far too clean to have been worn continually for twenty-eight days, as was claimed. Eleven people wrote from Coombe Bisset to state that they had seen "an old scrow-faced odd-looking woman" telling fortunes in exchange for money and ale. One complained that she had cheated him out of 6d., for which he wished her to be hanged!

Sir Crisp presented the new evidence to the attorney general and obtained a six-week stay of execution for Mary Squires. Elizabeth Canning, meanwhile, was dropped like a hot brick by her original lawyer, Mr Salt, but the Aldermanbury folk soon found her an enthusiastic replacement in Mr John Miles. Having first obtained her release on bail following her arrest for perjury, he then set about finding evidence to counteract the gypsy's alibi. There were plenty of people at Enfield Wash who remembered seeing Mary Squires in the area, and some at a time when she claimed to have been in Dorset. Loomworth Dane, landlord of the Bell at Enfield Highway, remembered the wind blowing up her gown as she passed him on January 5. Others were convinced they had seen the gypsies at Enfield as early as December. Miles collected these witnesses together and carted them off to Newgate to identify the gypsy. He also interviewed

45

a turnpike keeper who thought he had seen Canning with two men on the Hertford road; and others who thought they had seen her in a distressed state on the way back four weeks later. He talked to yet others who claimed that Wells or Squires had confessed to them in gaol that Canning was at the Enfield house after all. He even led an armed posse to Dorset with warrants to apprehend Clarke and Gibbons. Gibbons managed to escape their clutches at Dorchester, thanks to a magistrate who spotted a flaw in the warrant, but Clarke was taken to London and held there while attempts were made to persuade him to alter his testimony. Happily for Mary Squires, he would not be persuaded.

Each allegation in the Canning affair was now matched by a counter allegation and on June 9 a grand jury decided that both Elizabeth and three men from Dorset should be tried for perjury—the former over her claim that Mary Squires was at Enfield on January 2, the latter for saying she was in their county. By way of preparation, Sir Crisp Gascoyne arranged for George Squires to re-trace the route of the alibi journey with the under-sheriff of Dorset. They went over the ground five times, seeking additional witnesses, and at Dorchester Mr Willis unearthed an unexpected piece of evidence in the form of Lucy Squires' letter to Clarke, written for her at Basingstoke but never successfully delivered to its proper destination. The letter bore the date January 18 but the last digit of the year was missing due to damage at the edge of the page.

Mr Miles managed to delay the case until September but then, as the trials were about to come on, he suddenly quit the case for want of payment due from the friends of his Aldermanbury client. He disappeared to Gloucestershire, taking most of the papers containing the pro-Canning evidence with him. A third lawyer was appointed, then a fourth, by which time the stay of execution for Mary Squires had turned into a free pardon (touchingly, the gypsy family went straight to the Lord Mayor and thanked him on their knees), the Dorset men accused of perjury had been acquitted, and Elizabeth Canning had gone into hiding. She finally emerged, but it was April 29, 1754, before her plea of not guilty to perjury was entered and her trial at the Old Bailey finally got under way.

William Davy, one of three prosecution counsel, began by revealing that the purpose of the Squires family's walk to the west country towards the end of 1752 was the conveyance of smuggled goods "such as they meet with in seaport towns, and sell again to people in the country". The question at issue, he said, was where they were on January 1 and 2 and when they arrived at Enfield Wash.

The first two witnesses were women from Dorset, and a frail-looking Mary Squires watched from an armchair as her son George followed them to the stand. Starting from the point of their arrival at the Red Lion, South Perrot, on December 29, 1752, he gave the court as long and detailed an account as he could manage of the family's movements between then and their arrival at Enfield Wash. At the conclusion of this description, Davy pointed to Elizabeth Canning in the dock and asked Squires if he had seen her at Mother Wells' house.

"No, I did not. I never saw her before we were taken up in my life, if I was to be racked to death," the gypsy replied. "I'll stand with a sword put to my heart if ever I saw her till she came in the chaise. We came there on a Wednesday and at the end of a week and a day my mother was taken up."

The story was backed up by a veritable army of other witnesses from Abbotsbury, Litton Cheney, and places on the route to London, including Gibbons, Arnold, Clarke, Ford, Andrew Wake the Exciseman (recently sacked for "writing at home instead of going abroad"), and a couple of Litton bell-ringers who remembered seeing Mary Squires on the night they rang in the new year. The landlord of the Sloop Aground at Ridgeway recalled that the party paid him with a waistcoat because they were short of money. He remembered the date of the visit because it coincided with Blandford Quarter Sessions, torrential rain and flooding, and the death of a horse to which George Squires had referred in his evidence.

The weather also stuck in the mind of the landlord of the Coach and Horses at Dorchester.

"On the 10th there was such a rain they could not pass along the road," he told the court. "The waters were so high they went through a neighbour's house and my stable the back way. The old woman took up her coats and went along through it. I saw her go along part of it. I did not see it all; I had no business to watch her. The young woman was carried over by the miller's boy on horseback."

Thomas Greville of the Lamb at Coombe Bisset was unable to appear this time, having died of the smallpox acquired during his last visit to the Old Bailey in the previous September. His sister gave evidence instead, but this time she caught the disease and she also was dead within the week. She was followed to the witness box, though not to the grave, by the writer of Lucy's dictated letter to Clarke, then by a woman who put up the Squires family at Brentford.

It was all convincing stuff and the evidence of the men from the Goldsmith's Hall on Day Two of the trial also did little to assist the Canning cause. They had doubted her story from the day of their visit to Enfield Wash and now they said so. But the mob outside the courtroom had no such doubts and their increasingly unruly behaviour—which included an attack on Sir Crisp Gascoyne—warranted a public reading of the Riot Act by his successor as Lord Mayor, Sir Thomas Rawlinson.

The trial was well into its third day before the defence opened their case. Again there were numerous witnesses and they included Elizabeth Canning's mother, her uncle and aunt Colley, her former employer Mr Lyon (the only member of the Goldsmith quartet to stay loyal), James Lord the apprentice, the likes of Wintlebury and Scarratt, and many who claimed to have seen the girl on the road or the gypsies about Enfield Wash in December or early January.

Scarratt faced a searching cross-examination from Davy and was forced to admit that he was acquainted with Mother Wells' house and had been there several times in the past. But he strongly denied suggestions that he had quarrelled with Wells and sworn revenge or that he was involved in Elizabeth's disappearance.

"I have heard that it should be alleged against me that I took the girl away," he said by way of denial.

The prosecution found Wintlebury equally interesting.

"Don't you subscribe towards the support of Canning?" asked Davy's colleague Mr Willes.

"No, sir," Wintlebury replied.

"Was there any intrigue between Scarratt and her?"

"No. She would hardly go to the door to speak to anybody. I believe here quite different from an intriguing person."

The trial lasted six days and it was well after midnight on the final day when the jury were finally allowed to retire. They returned almost two hours later to announce their conclusion: "Guilty of perjury, but not wilful and corrupt."

The Recorder shook his head, gravely.

"I cannot receive your verdict," he announced, "because it is partial. You must either find her guilty of the whole indictment, or else acquit her."

Had they been in court at the time, Elizabeth's lawyers might well have protested on a point of law. But they were not, so the jury retired again. They returned at 2.41 a.m. with a final verdict: "Guilty of wilful and corrupt perjury; recommended to mercy."

Mercy was all Elizabeth Canning could hope for now.

"I hope," she whispered, "that your Lordships will be favourable to me. I had no intent of swearing away the gypsy's life; what has been done was only defending myself. I desire to be considered unfortunate."

ELIZABETH CANNING,
Drawn from the Life, as fhe ftood at the Bar to receive her Sentence, in th
Seffion's-Houfe, in the *Old-Bailey*.

Elizabeth Canning receives her sentence at the Old Bailey.

"It is your particular happiness," pronounced the Recorder, "that you are in a country where severe and sanguinary laws are not so familiar; and though many may expect, and the court could in this case justify, the most severe and exemplary punishment which the law can inflict, yet you will soon be convinced that your sentence is in no degree adequate to the greatness of your offence. The judgement of this court, therefore is, that you shall be imprisoned in the gaol of Newgate for one month; and after the expiration of your imprisonment, you shall be transported to some of His Majesty's colonies or plantations in America for the term of seven years; and if within that term you return, and are found at large in any of His Majesty's dominions of Great Britain or Ireland, you shall suffer death as a felon without benefit of clergy."

Elizabeth Canning left the shores of her native land on board the *Myrtilla* on August 7, 1754, bound for Philadelphia. With her she took the not insubstantial sum collected for her by her friends and letters of recommendation to help her make her way in the New World. Having crossed the Atlantic, she found her way to Weathersfield, Connecticut, and moved in with a clergyman and his young English wife, for whom she did household chores. In 1756, she married John Treat, great-nephew of a former governor of Connecticut, and two years later bore him a son, Joseph Canning Treat, to be followed in 1761 by a daughter, Elizabeth. Later that year, one English newspaper reported that following the expiry of her seven-year transportation sentence, she had now returned to England to collect a legacy of £500 from a sympathizer. There is, however, no other evidence to support this claim and no further news appeared until June 1773, when it was reported that "last week died very suddenly, at Weathersfield, Mrs. Elizabeth Treat, wife of Mr. Treat, formerly the famous Elizabeth Canning."

The true story behind the events of January 1753 probably went into the Connecticut soil with her, if indeed she knew it herself. The whole saga had been steeped in mystery from the start and was destined to remain so. Even Mary Squires the gypsy had taken some secrets to the grave when she died in 1762 at the age of eighty. There can be no doubt that the gypsies' alibi was genuine. The evidence to support their claim that they were in Dorset at the pertinent time is utterly overwhelming. But how they came to be in South Perrot and the exact purpose of their ambling journey has never been revealed. And why was London's first citizen moved to go to such great lengths—and to earn personal unpopularity into the bargain—to save the life of an elderly gypsy woman? The Squires family were always unable or unwilling to give any information about their route before arriving at South Perrot, even in evidence. At the Old Bailey, George failed to name a single town they had passed through between Kent and South Perrot or a single inn they had stayed at.

"Really, sir, I hope you will excuse me, be pleased to excuse me; I cannot tell indeed; please to excuse me," was all he could say.

It may be that George genuinely could not remember where they had been before they reached South Perrot. He remembered the route after that well enough but, as he himself pointed out, he had been over the ground several times since and his memory was refreshed. Or perhaps the gypsies did have something to hide. It was openly admitted that they were involved in smuggling, which was rife throughout the 18th century, and it is not inconceivable that they had contraband contacts to protect. For smugglers, however, they seem to have got on extremely well with the opposition. Not only did they make friends with Mr Wake the Exciseman, but during his evidence George also referred—reluctantly, it seemed—to a creditor of his, one Mr Norman, a Customs tidewaiter, since deceased, and to a visit he made to his relative Samuel Squires, "who belongs to the Customs". Were the Squires family, as some writers have suggested, really Government double agents out to spy on the smugglers of Southern England? It would help to explain the level of support they received from official sources, though it ought also to be pointed out that it was by no means unknown for people in official places to be in league with smugglers, whose activities attracted the kind of public sympathy and practical support generally denied to other crimes.

The precise nature of the gypsies' business remains a mystery, but if their alibi was genuine, as it obviously was, just what did happen to their accuser during the first four weeks of 1753? Again, we can do little more than guess at the truth, as many have done before us, but it does seem that there may have been some truth mixed in with the lies she told about the gypsies. Was it coincidence, for example, that Mother Wells' loft contained a bed of hay and a chipped black jug like the one Elizabeth had described? Was it coincidence that boards had recently been nailed to the window through which she claimed she had escaped? Was it sheer luck which enabled her to give an accurate description of the view from the loft? Was there reason to disbelieve those who claimed to have seen her on the Hertford Road? In addition, there is one further piece of evidence concerning Elizabeth's alleged stay at Enfield Wash that did not come to light until some time after her conviction and sentence for perjury. It came from a shepherd who had once bought a dog from Mother Wells' son and now, lying very ill at Cheshunt, asked for a message to be sent to Elizabeth Canning.

"My new dog," he said, "would be ever rambling home to Wells'. On the 15th of January, by the new style, I went into Wells' to ask after the creature, and it snowing very hard, and being very stormy weather, I sat in the kitchen for a space to shelter myself. Judith Natus was sitting by. Presently she opened the stair-foot door. Hearing something in the room, I looked up and saw a woman in the workshop, shuffling about as if she was very cold and weak, and in a ragged condition, with no gown on, only a petticoat, and something dirty over her shoulders. Judy clapped the door to. 'What's the matter?' asks Sal Howit. 'Tis that bitch above stairs,' says Judy."

There is no doubt that Elizabeth had been half-starved and badly treated and if it was really at Mother Wells' house, then why did she choose to jeopardize her credibility by mixing lies with the truth? Some of her less charitable contemporaries suggested she had invented the story to cover up a birth or abortion, but the medical evidence produced in court asserted firmly that she had never borne a child and there appears to have been no evidence to dispute her own claim that her virtue was intact.

The possible involvement of Wintlebury and/or Scarratt cannot be discounted, for the former had employed the girl and lived under the same roof as her, providing ample opportunity for a relationship or simply lustful thoughts and intentions, while the latter was more familiar with Mother Wells and her house than he at first cared to admit. Perhaps the pair conceived a joint plan so that Wintlebury could have his wicked way and Scarratt his revenge for some past quarrel? Again, one can only speculate. But the men in question could not expect their victim to keep mum about their involvement.

Perhaps Elizabeth Canning's mental and physical health played their part in creating the confusion of her story. Perhaps her proneness to fits which sometimes left her helpless and senseless for several hours at a stretch contributed to her confused, incomplete, and inaccurate recall of events. Or perhaps she really did have something to hide.

4

The Coffin in the Crypt
The mystery of John Damer's death in 1776

According to official records, the Honourable John Damer committed suicide at a tavern in London on August 15, 1776. Thirty-two years old, the son of and heir to the Right Honourable Joseph Lord Milton, squire of Milton Abbas in Dorset and former Member of Parliament for Weymouth, apparently shot himself in the head after dining in the company of four women and a blind fiddler in a first-floor room. Four days later, the *Western Flying Post or Sherborne and Yeovil Mercury* reported that a "young gentleman, eldest son of Lord M___n, and heir to an estate of £30,000 per annum, put an end to his existence on Wednesday night last, at the Bedford Arms in Covent Garden. The coroner's jury sat on the body yesterday morning, and pronounced their verdict Lunacy. He has left a widow behind him, but fortunately no children to lament his loss."

The parish burial register for Milton Abbas records that Damer was interred there on August 21. Amid much wailing and funereal pomp, his remains were laid to rest in the family vaults beneath the north transept of the Abbey church. Or were they? Subsequent generations of villagers would certainly have disputed the suggestion. They always claimed that Damer not only survived his funeral but even that he was seen around the family home in later years. There is also reason to think that the coffin that today sits beneath the memorial to Lord and Lady Milton may contain something other than John Damer's bones.

The Damer family owed their considerable wealth largely to Lord Milton's great-uncle, also Joseph Damer. Born in 1630, he became a trusted associate of Oliver Cromwell and upon the restoration to the throne of Charles II, moved to Ireland and bought up large estates cheaply. He also became a successful merchant and moneylender and through these and other enterprises amassed a fortune that has been described as "incalculable". Long before his death in 1720 at the age of

Milton Abbey House in the 18th century.

ninety-one, he had earned himself such a reputation for penny-pinching that Jonathan Swift was prompted to describe him as the richest man in Ireland and the greatest miser. He left his riches to his two nephews, one of whom, John Damer's grandfather, purchased Winterborne Came, near Dorchester.

Joseph Milton, John's father, married extremely well, his bride being Caroline Sackville, daughter of the first Duke of Dorset. Joseph, as well as being a man of great wealth, was also one of great ambition and even greater ruthlessness. In 1752, ten years after his marriage, he bought Milton Abbey and put into operation an extraordinary scheme of demolition, development, and landscaping which was to transform the village and the valley in which it stood . This included the replacement of the old medieval house with a new building, the destruction of the old village, and the creation of a new village comprising forty double houses, each for two families. Today the cottages, with their striking white walls, neatly thatched roofs, and lawns running down to the main street of Milton Abbas, are hailed as one of the more picturesque sights of Dorset. But their first occupiers were less impressed as they were forced, regardless of their own wishes, to vacate their old homes when the leases expired and move to the new village created on the orders of their unpopular landlord.

The cottages were constructed during the 1770s and by the end of the decade all that remained of the old village were two houses and, outside the church wall, a schoolhouse and two inns. Both surviving houses belonged to William Harrison, a Blandford lawyer who knew his rights and refused to budge. Lord Milton, seeking to complement his newly created gentleman's mansion and country park with an ornamental lake, ordered the sluice gates at the old abbey pond to be opened, causing in the process both the stream running through the park and one of Harrison's houses to be flooded. Harrison was moved only to take Lord Milton to court, where he won the case. Soon afterwards, it is said, the squire mistook the ringing of the abbey bells in celebration of Guy Fawkes day as a celebration by the villagers of his legal defeat. He ordered the removal of the offending bells, which were carried away on wagons as the astonished parishioners looked on. He remained unable to remove Harrison, however, until the lawyer passed away in his own good time, at which stage the park was completed.

Lord Milton, who was made Earl of Dorchester a few years before his death in 1798, fathered four children, John, born in 1744, George, Lionel, and Caroline, but although all four survived to adulthood and the last three survived him, they all died childless and the estate passed to another branch of the family and was eventually sold. Lady Caroline, Lord Milton's wife, died in 1775, the year before the reputed death of their eldest son.

Like his father, John Damer married well, at least by the standards of 18th-century high society, which tended to measure such matters in terms of wealth and social standing rather than personal compatibility. His bride was Anne Seymour Conway a young lady of refined temperament and great artistic talent, the only child of the Right Honourable Henry Seymour Conway, of Sundridge, Kent, and his wife, Caroline, Countess of Ailesbury. Anne's father was both a military man and a politician, reaching the rank of General and later Field Marshall in the former career and becoming successively a Member of Parliament, Secretary of State for the Northern Department, Privy Council member, and Governor of Jersey in the latter.

Anne was in her 18th year when she married Damer, a man five years her senior, at Park Place in the parish of Remenham on Sunday June 14, 1767, and it was an event that pleased both families and others besides. Horace Walpole, a cousin of the bride, who was eventually to inherit his Strawberry Hill estate at Richmond, wrote to Sir Horace Mann a few weeks before the wedding, "Mr. Conway is in great felicity going to marry his only daughter to Lord Milton's eldest son. The estate in Lord Milton's possession is already £23,000 a year, seven more just coming from the author of their wealth, an old uncle in Ireland. Lord Milton gives £5,000 a year and settles the rest. Miss Conway is to have a jointure of £2,500 a year and £500 pin-money."

Another close associate of the family, Lady Mary Coke, observed that "Miss Conway's fortune is £10,000, which goes in jewels, equipages and furniture." A few days after the wedding, she adds: "Lady Ailesbury came to town yesterday with Mr. and Mrs. Damer; she laments the Court being in mourning, as it prevents her finery being seen; I think it has been the case of most brides this year."

At first the young couple made the most of their riches. They paid several visits to Damer's family home at Milton Abbey House and also stayed with Anne's parents when they were at Park Place. And as Anne's biographer, Percy Noble, writes, they "soon went a great deal into society, living a most extravagant life, and entertaining at their house in Tilney Street the great world of fashion, literature and art." To all but the most astute observers, it appeared to be an auspicious beginning to a union of great promise.

As time went on, however, it became apparent that all was not as it should be in the relationship. Increasingly, Anne began to appear at entertainments without her husband, sometimes alone, sometimes with her mother. Damer complained that his wife was rarely at home, but he for his part had turned his attention to his own favourite pursuits of horse racing and gambling, which held no appeal whatsoever for Mrs Damer. Like his two brothers, Damer was a notorious spendthrift and his debts mounted as he borrowed more and more from Jewish moneylenders—a curious irony when one considers how the family fortune was acquired.

"Mr Damer's chief grievance against his wife was that she was constantly away from home, but he seems to have been a difficult person to live with," writes Noble. "Heir to a fortune of not less than £30,000 a year, which he seemed bent on squandering before it came to him, he was one of a wild, foolish set about London, whose whole glory in life was centred in the curl of a coat-collar and the brim of a hat. These young fops made up for want of wit by the most extravagant display of ridiculous eccentricity; their chief delight seems to have been to astonish their friends, and Damer found an added satisfaction in thus annoying his amiable wife. He appeared three times a day in a new suit. The extent of his wardrobe may be imagined from the statement that at his death it was sold for £15,000, which appears a large amount for even one so extravagant, but it must be remembered that these were the days of silk, lace and embroidery, and that men's clothes then could cost as much as or even more than did those of the ladies."

In 1775, Mrs Damer returned from a visit to Paris to announce that she had decided to separate from her husband, a move which must, in Percy Noble's view, have been "most galling" to a woman of her "refined and delicate temperament, brought up as she had been by such devoted parents, with such a careful moral training from her earliest childhood." Neither was it a step which met with widespread general approval, although Lady Sarah Lennox, a beautiful young society woman who had taken a similar step in 1769, observed: "I think one has no right to blame her more than him; he had no business to marry a girl he did not like, than she to accept a man she was totally indifferent to, and he was as much to blame in giving her the example of never living at home, as she was to make all her life opposite to his. In short, I cannot think it fair to blame one more than the other, but as it is evident that love was out of the question, I must give her credit for her present conduct."

John Damer's extravagant lifestyle continued unabated. By the summer of 1776 his debts totalled more than £70,000, a fortune by most 18th-century standards. Lord Milton, saddled as he was with three free-spending sons each seemingly intent on eating into his balances, refused to bail out his eldest or even to see him. General Conway, now suffering from a temporary attack of facial paralysis said to have been brought on by the worry of his daughter's foundering marriage, was probably in no position to help, being already committed to the costly task of beautifying his estate at Park Place. (His £10,000 settlement upon his daughter had already been absorbed by her estranged husband's excesses.) John Damer had drained his sources dry and his creditors were closing in. He was trapped in a prison of his own making and, in Noble's words, "formed the unhappy resolve of depriving himself of existence". At 3 a.m. on August 15, 1776, he put the barrel of a pistol to his head in a first-floor room at the Bedford Arms tavern, Covent Garden, and squeezed the trigger. Or did he?

The inquest into Damer's death was held at the Bedford Arms at 6 p.m. the same day before the local coroner, Mr Thomas Prickard, and a jury of twenty-two "able and sufficient men" of the liberty of Westminster. They heard evidence from only three witnesses, the first being vintner John Robinson, landlord of the Bedford Arms, who told how, between 7 and 8 o'clock the previous evening, he received a note from Damer directing him to prepare a supper for him, to be ready at 10 o'clock, and also requesting the presence of a fiddler called Burnet and some ladies, "in particular a little Miss Richmond that sings". Robinson said he had received several notes from Damer before but this one was written in a "confused manner" and "not like his usual manner of writing".

The official record of the inquest continues: "The deponent . . . . says that a little after 11 o'clock the deceased came there and supped in the room on the first floor with four women, Burnet, a blind fiddler, being in the room playing on the violin; says that the deceased eat very little if any; says that the women sung after supper and stayed with the deceased until about three o'clock this morning, when deceased ordered this deponent to tell the women to go out of the room and to give a guinea to each of them, which deponent did accordingly, and the four women went away, Burnet the fiddler staying in the room with the deceased; says that in a few minutes Burnet came downstairs, saying that the deceased had ordered him to go down and would send for him again in a quarter-of-an-hour; says that Burnet in about 20 minutes went up-stairs and returned immediately saying that there was a disagreeable smell in the room where the deceased was and supposed the candles were fallen down, upon which deponent went upstairs into deceased's room which smelt very strongly of gunpowder."

Robinson went on to describe the scene that confronted him as he entered the room. "The deceased was sitting in a chair, bleeding from a wound on the right side of his head, his clothes being bloody and much blood upon the floor; says that he felt the deceased's hand which was not cold but he observed no signs of life in the deceased; says that he believes the deceased's death was caused by the wound on the deceased's head as abovementioned and that he gave it to himself by discharging a loaded pistol against his head, and that he this deponent then found a pistol upon the floor between the deceased's feet, which appeared to have been discharged, the cock being down."

The licensee said Damer had been a customer of his tavern for many years but that his behaviour on this occasion was "very different from what it used to be, making this deponent put the deceased's hat upon the fiddler's head, and says that the deceased did not then appear to be intoxicated with liquor".

The blind fiddler identified himself as Richard Burnet, of Exeter Court, Strand, and summarized events from the time when he received a message summoning him to the Bedford Arms to the moment of his return to the silent room, when Damer failed to speak to him and his nostrils detected the disagreeable smell that he thought at the time was caused by a candle having fallen over. He informed Mr Robinson, who went to investigate and returned immediately, saying "Oh my God! He has shot himself."

Burnet told the inquest that throughout the period when Damer was left alone, he heard no noise from upstairs, neither the report of a pistol nor the sound of anyone else going up there. Like Robinson, he did, however, comment on certain aspects of the dead man's behaviour. "Mr Damer," says the coroner's record, "before supper put his hat twice upon deponent's head, bidding deponent keep it on, and on deponent thanking deceased, he said that he did not mean to give it him; and says that Mr Damer afterwards ordered Mr Robinson to put the deceased's hat upon deponent's head, which he never had done before; and deponent thought that the deceased was not so cheerful that night as he had been before when deponent attended him, and deponent says that the deceased was not intoxicated with liquor last night."

The third and final witness, Damer's house steward, John Armitage, made only a brief testimony, saying that he had lived with the dead man for nine years, that he had frequently had occasion to apply to him for money and that he had last done so two days before, when Damer gave him a note for £26 5s. for the use of the house. Armitage added that Damer has "for some time past appeared to be uneasy and disturbed in his mind and that his spirits were oppressed, but deponent cannot account for it".

After due consideration, the jury arrived at their verdict, namely that John Damer, "not being of sound mind, memory and understanding but lunatic and distracted," had held a pistol "loaded with gunpowder and a leaden bullet" to the right side of his head and inflicted a mortal wound to himself by discharging the weapon. (Lunacy verdicts were common in such cases because the alternative—felonius suicide—meant that the victim's goods, chattels, and lands had to be forfeited and his body buried under a highway in unhallowed ground.) The jury also concluded that Damer's death was instantaneous.

It was not unusual in 18th-century England to hold an inquest within hours of a sudden death, but there do seem to be three fairly serious omissions from the evidence presented in this case. Firstly, although there must have been plenty of potential witnesses concerning Damer's financial predicament, none were called and the likely motive for suicide was hardly even hinted at, Armitage the house steward saying he could not account for his employer's disturbed state of mind. Secondly, although the coroner records that no one heard the pistol go off, it is not clear from his record, as it is in a letter written by Horace Walpole five days later, that "the ball had not gone through his head". Thirdly, there appears to have been no mention of a scrap of paper which, according to Walpole, was found on a table nearby and bore the words, "The people of the house are not to blame for what has happened, which was my own act." Walpole describes the note as "the sole tribute he [Damer] paid to justice and decency", adding, "What a catastrophe for a man of 32, heir to two-and-twenty thousand a year. We are persuaded that lunacy, not distress, was the sole cause of his fate."

Like Horace Walpole, the *Western Flying Post* seems to have been somewhat better informed than the coroner. On August 26, the west-country newspaper reported: "We hear that the cause of the unfortunate Mr D . . . was as follows: Having at different times lately lost, and granted annuities to the amount of £80,000 and being much pressed for the money, he wrote to his father, laying a state of his embarrassed affairs before him; but the father, who some time since paid of a large sum for him, peremptorily refused. He then wrote to his relation, Lord G.G., who gave him but little hopes, at the same time that he made a private application to the father, who was partly prevailed upon to settle his affairs. Young Mr D . . ., however, being ignorant of this, took the unhappy resolution of cancelling all his debts, by paying the great debt of nature, which he accomplished on Thursday evening last. He has left a disconsolate widow behind him, the daughter of General C . . ., whom he married a few years ago, but left no children."

News of Damer's death spread quickly and sent shockwaves through the upper echelons of English society. Writing to George Selwyn on August 17, Lord Carlisle said: "A coroner's inquest sat on Mr Damer's body and a verdict of lunacy was returned. What were Mr Damer's motives for so dreadful an action? There was no man more indifferent to me, but the account shocked me extremely. It is a bad example to others in misery. It makes people think of having recourse to that method of finishing their calamities, without which, perhaps, it had never entered their heads. If it was not so selfish an action, it would be difficult to condemn it in some cases. There never appeared anything like madness in him, yet the company he kept seemed indeed but a bad preparation for eternity."

The Honourable Thomas Townshend, also writing to George Selwyn on the same date, said: "Mary was in some measure prepared for the melancholy story of Mr Damer's death, as we had last night some account (though a less circumstantiated one than you give) of that terrible and shocking event. We all feel extremely for what Lord Milton particularly must suffer for the loss of a son (whom he had upon the whole so much reason to esteem and to love) in so deplorable a way."

Though he may have been suffering within, the attitude of the dead man's father following the tragedy proved almost as shocking to some as did the event itself. "Lord Milton, whom nothing can soften," wrote Walpole, "wreaks his fury on Mrs Damer, though she deserves only pity and shows no resentment. He insists on selling her jewels, this is all the hurt he can do her."

Lady Sarah Lennox, writing to Lady Susan O'Brien on September 19, was even more vehement. "I am provoked at Lord Milton," she said, "for I was throwing away my pity for him, and behold, not even the death of his son has softened him about his family in general, or taught him generosity. He has been very shabby about Lionel Damer, and quite brutal to Mrs Damer who, by the way, behaves with all propriety in the world; when one commends a widow for behaving well, it is allowing that love was out of the question, which is to be sure in her case. Lord Milton has taken her diamonds, furniture, carriages, and everything away to pay the debts with, and he abused her for staying in another man's house (for she stayed a few days there before she went to the country, and the house is another's being seized). Upon hearing this she left it, and chose to go in a hackney coach, taking only her inkstand, a few books, her dog, and her maid with her, out of that fine house. I think it was spirited and noble in her; she had three guineas in her pocket, which were to last her till Michaelmas, for Lord Milton did not offer her any assistance. Her sister, as you may imagine, attended her and gave her money, and she went to Mr Conway's house; she is to live with him for a year in order to save one year's income (£2,500) which she gives towards the payment of Mr Damer's debts, which cannot be quite paid by the sale of everything even."

The letter goes on: "The poor servants are owed 14 months' wages, which I think one of the most melancholy reflections, for you see that they are in absolute want of bread, if they are unlucky in not getting a place immediately. She paid (out of the Duchess's money) those servants who were in immediate want, the rest were too generous to take any, and refused absolutely to take more than would serve them for immediate use; they are all fond of her and cried bitterly at her leaving the house, in such a way too, but the Damers tell me she walked through the house amidst them all, into a hackney coach, with a firmness that is quite heroic, for though she may be accused of not loving her husband, she cannot be accused of not loving her house and all its grandeur."

Anne Damer was comforted by those close to her but, not surprisingly, her health suffered for a time. The widow was supposed to receive a jointure of £2,500 a year from her father-in-law but

Anne, wife of John Damer.

voluntarily sacrificed the first year's payment to help pay off her husband's debts, then found that subsequent payments did not arrive as regularly as she was entitled to expect. By 1780, four years after her husband's death, she was forced to ask the man responsible for managing her finances to harry Lord Milton, for "I have not had any money sent for some time, and people are so pressing with me to be paid that I do not know what to do". In the long term, however, childless widowhood appears to have given Anne the opportunity to enjoy the kind of cultured life style that came naturally to her and on which she clearly thrived. She went on to live a long and eventful life, travelling widely in Europe and counting many of the most eminent royal, political, military, literary, and artistic figures of her generation among her friends and acquaintances. She took a great interest in the theatre, acting in a number of dramatic productions, and became one of the most respected sculptors of her day, her works including a bust of Lord Nelson, which subsequently found its way to the British Museum. Once she had recovered from the shock of her husband's death, her life, according to Percy Noble, seems to have been "unclouded by any troubles except the deaths of her beloved parents". She died peacefully on May 28, 1828, in her eightieth year and was buried at Sundridge church.

But what of the mystery surrounding her husband's alleged suicide? Did he really put a loaded pistol to his head and squeeze the trigger as a coroner's jury concluded he had done? Or did he somehow fake his death to deceive his creditors and reappear on his family's country estate at some later date as the inhabitants of Milton Abbas always claimed? The contemporary evidence to support the latter theory is certainly not great. The coroner's inquest into his death was not as thorough as it might have been, but that was not unusual for the 18th century and does not in itself show that there was some conspiracy afoot. On the other hand, it does seem odd that no pistol shot was heard either by the landlord of the Bedford Arms or by the blind fiddler, whose hearing was presumably fairly acute. It is also odd that the ball, according to Horace Walpole, did not penetrate Damer's head and that the coroner's jury were informed neither of this nor of the suicide note that Walpole said he had left.

If Damer did fake his death to escape his debts, as has been suggested, he would presumably have needed at least one accomplice and possibly more. It was normal in those days for a jury as well as the coroner to view the body and examine any injuries before reaching their verdict and the inquest documents and other contemporary accounts suggest that this was the case at the Bedford Arms. Since it is hardly conceivable that the coroner and all his twenty-two jurors were involved in a conspiracy, then one must assume that there was a genuine corpse for them to view and that it had a head wound. However, assuming that neither the coroner nor any of the jurors knew Damer when he was alive, and since the fiddler was blind, it appears there were only two people present who were in a position to identify the body - Robinson, the landlord, and Armitage, Damer's house steward. Both had known Damer for years and had served him regularly in their respective roles. It is not inconceivable that they could have co-operated in some elaborate scheme thought up by Damer to fake his own death - a scheme that almost certainly, would have involved the acquisition of a body other than his. This, in 18th century London, would not have been as difficult as it sounds, especially if the body was "borrowed" to be returned later.

All this, of course, is pure speculation. It certainly does not amount to a prima facie case in support of the claim that Damer survived and most investigators would probably dismiss the suggestion as being no more than 18th-century village tittle-tattle with no likely basis in fact. There is, however, one piece of evidence that ensures that the Damer file cannot yet be closed.

In or about the year 1873, Mr Frederick Fane, of Moyles Court, Fordingbridge, was staying at Milton Abbey when he heard the legend of John Damer, with some minor variations. Describing the occasion at a meeting of the Dorset Natural History andAntiquarian Field Club more than twenty years later, he recalled that at the time of his visit some repairs were being carried out on the north transept of the Abbey church. "While waiting about one morning, for breakfast, I strolled into the Abbey, and entered into conversation with the clerk of the works, superintending the repairs. He told me that there had always existed a tradition, in the parish of Milton, that nearly or quite a hundred years previously when, as you are aware, the village stood on the ground adjacent to the Abbey, where the flower garden now is, and the Abbey was the parish church, a bogus funeral had taken place there. One of the young Damers, a son of the Lord Milton of the time, had been extravagant, and his presence had been much required by the bailiffs, and he had escaped a search made for him by them at Milton on various occasions. One day, a message arrived at Milton that the young man had died on the continent and was to be brought over for burial there.

"This was accordingly done and a more than usual display was made at the funeral, even exceeding the displays common at the time. He was buried in the vaults of Lord Milton, below the north transept of the

Abbey Church, and immediately beneath that lovely monument to Lord and Lady Milton, which is probably well known to most of us here. However, the country people were not without suspicions, would not and did not believe that young Damer was really dead and buried, and it was believed that on many occasions subsequently he was seen in the flesh about his paternal home. At any rate, his apparent death and burial appear to have satisfied his anxious creditors that nothing farther was to be expected from him in liquidation of his debts. The people of Milton said nothing but thought a good deal no doubt."

During the conversation, the clerk of the works mentioned to Fane that it had been necessary to open the flooring of the transept and that in doing so they had come across the entrance to the Milton vaults. He invited the visitor to follow him down the stairway into the vaults, where he would see something that would convince him of the truth of the Damer legend.

"Descending the stairs," Fane told his fellow naturalists and archaeologists, "I found, as well as I can recollect, three or at any rate two, considerable open vaults with numerous coffins, upon tressels, upon each side of a central passage, some covered with tattered velvet, and pasteboard property coronets lying on their tops – a very singular sight. In the farthest vault was a coffin with the brass nameplate, which had been attached to the outer case, still lying on the minor leaden one, bearing an inscription detailing the name of a Damer, who appeared to have died, at a little more than 20 (sic) years of age, somewhere about 1770."

The clerk of the works invited Fane to lift the coffin as it lay on the trestles.

"This I found impossible owing to its extraordinary weight," the gentleman recalled.

"Now, sir, try to lift this one," said the clerk, pointing to another nearby.

The second coffin came up "without the slightest exertion".

"There, sir, this one contains a body gone to dust," the clerk went on. "The other one is full of stones, as it was supposed by the old villagers would be the case if any opportunity ever again occurred for investigation."

As soon as the construction work was completed, the vaults at Milton Abbey were sealed off again and the coffin and its contents left to sit undisturbed on their trestles indefinitely. Perhaps one day circumstances will conspire to make possible the opening of the vaults once again and even of the coffin. Unless and until they do, the truth behind the legend of John Damer's death will remain a mystery.

5

The Tarrant Valley Vampire
The mystery of a steward's suicide, 1786

According to tradition, the ghost of William Doggett can be recognized by the ribbons of yellow silk that tie in his breeches at the knee. The one-time steward of Eastbury House, Tarrant Gunville, is said to appear headless as he drives around the park in a spectral coach and four, contemplating the lost grandeur of a house that was once one of the finest in England. There is talk, too, of Doggett being a vampire come back to haunt the village, where his body is supposed to have been dug up sixty years after his death and found not to have decomposed. In the surviving wing of Eastbury House itself, stories are told of doors that open themselves and of the sounds of an invisible person moving about. Some have refused to sleep in the room where Doggett is reputed to have shot himself dead two centuries ago after cheating his employer out of thousands of pounds.

Tarrant Gunville is on the fringes of Cranborne Chase, formerly a royal hunting forest and, later, a resort of criminals and fugitives of every kind. Many true-life dramas have been enacted there down the centuries, leaving a legacy today of intermingled fact and fiction that are often difficult to separate. The ghost of the ill-fated Duke of Monmouth is said to have appeared in a cottage, now demolished, at Woodyates, where he stopped for a change of clothing not long before his capture a few miles away at Horton Heath in 1685. The ghost of a deer-poacher's hand, severed in a battle with gamekeepers on Chettle Common in 1780, apparently leaves its Pimperne grave at night to haunt Bussey Stool Walk, Tarrant Gunville, in search of its owner.

The tale of William Doggett is of a similar kind, for he really did exist and he really was the steward at Eastbury House, but the true facts about him are not easy to unravel. Most published accounts associate him with a former squire of Tarrant Gunville, George Bubb Dodington, the first Baron Melcombe, a man often seen as one who

Eastbury House in its heyday.

most perfectly encapsulated the opulence and extravagance of 18th-century England. "The most swollen figure of a diseased political age," F. J. Harvey Darton calls him, in a reference which could be taken as relating to his bank balance, his social and political ambitions, or his physical shape, or perhaps all three and other characteristics besides.

Born at Weymouth, Dodington began life as plain George Bubb, son of a humble apothecary, but in 1720, when he was twenty-nine, he inherited a fortune from his uncle, George Dodington, whose name he also adopted. The late Mr Dodington had recently commenced work on a palatial home at Tarrant Gunville, designed by Sir John Vanbrugh on a scale to rival Castle Howard and Blenheim, and his nephew, already MP for Winchelsea and Britain's Envoy Extraordinary to the Court of Spain, was just the man to continue the task. Over a fourteen-year period, he spent £140,000 on completing the house and ensuring that it would compare with almost any in the land.

Eastbury House, Hutchins' *History . . . of Dorset* tells us, was "one of the grandest and most superb in this county, and indeed in the kingdom," with gardens that were "very extensive and beautiful," "adorned with vistas and plantations of trees" and with "canals supplied by an engine worked by horses." The main part of the house alone had a frontage extending 144 feet and was adjoined by arcades, offices, and other buildings that extended the distance to 570 feet. "These buildings being of different heights, and the turrets at each corner of the house, with the Venetian windows, rising above the rest, give the whole structure a very grand appearance."

The house, standing in a park five miles round and including most of Tarrant Hinton and Tarrant Monkton and parts of several other parishes, featured a "magnificent hall," sumptuously decorated and adorned with statues and busts. At one end of it were "three noble apartments, one hung with crimson velvet, another with flowered velvet, a third with satin, all richly laced with gold."

It was in these luxurious surroundings that the flamboyant George Bubb Dodington held court and where, according to one visitor, he was "not to be approached but through a suite of apartments and was rarely seated but under painted ceilings and gold entablatures." In the political field, his associates included such eminent statesmen as Walpole, Pelham, and Frederick, Prince of Wales, even when, on occasions, they were opposing each other; but his seat at Eastbury is more noted for the impressive list of literary figures whom he entertained there, among them the novelist Henry Fielding and the most famous writer in Europe at that time, Voltaire.

Dodington received his longed-for peerage in 1761 and died the following year, married but childless save for the son of a mistress, whose illegitimacy meant that he did not qualify to inherit the estate. Instead it passed by a family settlement to his relative, Richard, Earl Temple, and hence to George, the second Earl Temple, created Marquis of Buckingham in 1784. They found the maintenance of such grandeur impossibly expensive and in 1763 the furniture was sold off piecemeal. At one point they even offered £200 a year to anyone willing to live at Eastbury, but eventually most of the house and ancillary buildings were pulled down.

It was during the heady days of Lord Melcombe's occupation, however, that William Doggett is alleged to have performed his duties as steward to one of the most successful social climbers of the age. He was, Christina Hole tells us in her book *Haunted England,* "Lord Melcombe's steward at the time when building was going on. He is said to have borrowed large sums from his employer in order to help a brother in difficulties. When repayment was demanded, he could not find the money and he appropriated some of the building materials to raise funds. Probably he hoped to pay everything back later on, but he was not given enough time. Lord Melcome suddenly announced his

Eastbury in the 18th century showing the massive central elevation.

intention of coming to Tarrant Gunville earlier than was expected, and the wretched steward shot himself on hearing the news. His blood is said to have left a stain on the floor which could never afterwards be effaced."

Rodney Legg takes us a step further in *Mysterious Dorset*. In the village pub, named the Bugle Horn after the Dodington Crest, the locals believed that "Doggett was un-dead, who unworthy of burial in consecrated ground would live on as a vampire to emerge from his tomb at night to drink the blood of sleeping villagers. Their story in justification of this is that when the parish church at Tarrant Gunville was demolished in the 19th century Doggett's corpse was found not to have decomposed and the legs were bound together with a ribbon of yellow silk."

These accounts, and others like them, appear to derive from an article published towards the end of the 19th century, a copy of which has been pasted into an old book of vestry minutes by a long-departed rector of Tarrant Gunville. The article tells us that "Bubb Dodington had a trusted steward and agent of the name of Dogget, and this man — to help a speculative brother, it is said — began, when Eastbury was in the full zenith of its splendour, to help himself extensively to his master's property. It is believed that about the time that the impetuous

Bubb had determined to destroy the house, he made such a resolve because he had discovered how deceived he had been in a servant of many years."

The article continues: "Be this as it may, Dogget managed to evade a full settlement with his injured master till the mansion had been almost pulled down, and then it seems that the rascally steward daily expected his master and a solicitor to appear on the spot. Dogget had even drawn and spent certain of the money paid for the very building materials heaped up by the wreckers, and he, one day, when Lord Melcombe was coming back for a reckoning, went into one of the beautiful dismantled rooms of the remaining wing and shot himself. His blood is said to be still visible on the white marble floor."

Whether William Doggett really was employed by Lord Melcombe is uncertain—the record of his marriage to Mrs Elizabeth Dean of Corfe Mullen in 1753 offers no suggestion of a connection with Tarrant Gunville at that time. The ceremony took place at Winterborne Houghton and Doggett's home parish is given as Milton Abbas. Elizabeth and William Doggett do appear in the Tarrant Gunville parish register eventually—on the occasions of their burials on June 24, 1785, and June 23, 1786, respectively — but this was a full quarter-of-a-century after the demise of Lord Melcombe. There are also two Doggett marriages recorded at Tarrant Gunville — of Elizabeth Doggett to Christopher Fleet in 1794 and Ann Doggett to Roger Clavill the following year.

The traditional association of Doggett with the first Baron Melcombe must, therefore, be questionable, but that does not necessarily mean that the tale is false in its entirety. Mr Peter Farquharson, of Wimborne, whose family have owned the surviving parts of Eastbury since 1807 and who was born in the house in 1909, was brought up with a variation of the Doggett story that is not only feasible but which, he insists, is truth rather than legend. The Farquharson version ignores Lord Melcombe altogether and places Doggett as steward to the second Lord Temple, later Marquis of Buckingham, who owned Eastbury in the 1780s.

"The story I have known all my life," Mr Farquharson tells me, "is that Lord Temple had developed tuberculosis and gone to Italy and that from there he wrote to Doggett telling him to pull down the wings of the house but to leave the main house standing. But Doggett believed that his master, on account of his health, would never return and instead of just demolishing the wings he began systematically to pull the whole house down, starting with the south wing and then coming across to the main house. As the work progressed, he sold off the materials to all sorts of other houses including, I believe, Bryanston."

Like most other versions of the tale, this account includes the unexpected return of the Lord and master.

"Doggett got wind that he was on his way home, realized what would happen and went off on a binge and committed suicide," says Mr Farquharson. "He went off in the coach, drinking like mad, then came back up the drive again, went into the green room and shot himself."

Corroborative evidence for this version of events is to be found in the same book of 19th-century vestry minutes in which have been pasted the Victorian article on the subject. Some notes in the hand of the Rev William Henry Hitchcock, who was rector of Tarrant Gunville from 1889 to 1900, refer to the appearance of William Doggett's name in the burial register in 1786 and tell us: "A strange story is told of a suicide; and burial in church porch of a steward to Eastbury of this name and date! That in the constant absence of the then owner, Duke of Buckingham, he took upon himself to pull down large portions of Eastbury House and other houses were built of the materials. At last tidings of the same spoilation reached the Duke's ears, and on his coming to inspect for himself, the steward Doggett blew his brains out; the woodwork of the room bearing the marks of blood when restored to Mr. Farquharson (from whom I had this history July 1889. W. H. W.)."

A further note, added later, names Bryanston House, Tarrant Gunville rectory, and the Manor House at Ashmore as being among the buildings that incorporate stone from Doggett's profit-making vandalism.

The Farquharson-Hitchcock version appears to be the earliest traceable source of the story and it also fits the evidence better than others. Contrary to the claims of some writers, the demolition of Eastbury was not begun in Lord Melcombe's time (he would surely have found the very idea unthinkable) and it was still standing when the first edition of Hutchins' *History . . . of Dorset* was published in 1774. Neither did the demolition occur, as has also been suggested, in 1788, by which time William Doggett had been dead two years. There may still have been demolition work going on in 1788, for the destruction of a stately home was no five-minute task but, as we learn from the diary of John Byng, who interrupted his travels for a look at Eastbury in 1782, the house was at that time being destroyed. This was almost certainly within Doggett's period of stewardship and gives him a full four years of stone-selling before he put an end to himself in 1786.

Eastbury under demolition in the 1780s.

This does not, of course, conclusively prove the truth behind the legend of Doggett's death but it does go a long way towards it. Unfortunately no inquest documents, which might have illuminated the matter further, appear to survive.

But what of the other elements of this masterpiece of village tradition? What of the bloodstains on the floor where Doggett shot himself in 1786? What of the headless spectre riding madly around the park in a coach and four? What of claims that the old steward's corpse had failed to decompose after sixty years in the grave?

Of the bloodstains on the floor, we can, perhaps, swiftly dispose, for Mr Peter Farquharson reveals with a grin: "My father used to put a little red ink down by the fireplace in the green room, then tell people it was the blood of William Doggett, which had never gone!"

The ghost stories are less easily dealt with.

"I haven't seen the ghost myself," says Mr Farquharson, "but I admit that I'm a coward and it would terrify me. I would not sleep in the green room myself and I know others who would never stay there. I knew an actress who stayed there once and swore that she had seen a ghost. And during the war three nurses came down from Liverpool, arriving in the middle of the night, and were put in the room, and at 4 or 4.30 in the morning they were out on the landing saying they couldn't sleep there. Then there was the little black spaniel I had with me as I was going to bed one night. He must have seen something that terrified him because he suddenly stopped on the stairs and just wouldn't move."

The story about the exhumation of Doggett is even more mysterious. Peter Farquharson has never heard the tale and the Rev. Hitchcock, although pondering on the burial of a suicide in consecrated ground ("How could a suicide be buried by the church, and in the porch?" he asks) makes no mention of it in his notes. Yet Richard Sale, one of the few modern writers to associate Doggett correctly with Lord Temple rather than Lord Melcombe, tells us with an air of certainty that "the coffin was opened and to the horror of the exhumers Doggett was found to be rosy cheeked, his body totally whole, no sign of decomposition. And, around his knees, there were yellow silk ribbons. The locals were convinced that he was a vampire — how else could he still be fresh? — but it is not recorded that they drove a stake into his heart."

That Doggett's tomb in the porch was interfered with is certainly a possibility for, as the vestry minute book informs us, it was found in March 1844 to be "absolutely necessary that the ground should be lowered from the porch round the tower to the North side of the church opposite the porch." The work, which effectively meant the rebuilding of the church, was duly approved and carried out and the building was reconsecrated in the late summer or autumn of 1845. But of the discovery of a well-preserved corpse, no contemporary mention has been found and, until it is, this aspect at least of the Doggett saga must remain a mystery unsolved.

6

The Witch and the Parson

The mystery of Susan Woodrow and the Rector of Turnerspuddle, 1804-5

It is hard to find a more remote representative of rural Dorset than Turnerspuddle, which squats serenely beside the River Piddle a mile or two southwest of Bere Regis. Originally called Toner's Piddle after the family of de Toneres, who were lords of the manor in Norman times, it gives the impression of having changed but little in the intervening centuries. Its cottages and farm buildings, struggling to number in double figures between them, boast a single tarmac road, which divides itself near the parish church into an unmetalled bridleway and a swampy track. The latter offers a choice of fords or footbridges to the traveller wishing to cross the Piddle and a tributary to reach the hamlet of Throop; the former heads determinedly westwards towards its famous neighbour of Tolpuddle. The church itself, always humble, has become the more so since it fell into disuse some years ago.

The striking remoteness of Turnerspuddle is not a new phenomenon and generations of writers have been moved either to comment on it or to ignore the village completely. Olive M. Philpott, arriving in the 1940s in search of inspiration for an article for the *Dorset Year Book,* described it as a "little lost hamlet, with a ghostly church standing greyly amongst the pale willows at the water's edge and half-a-score of old cottages timidly approaching the road, with a bewildered air, as if wondering how they, that so obviously belonged to the 17th century, happened to find themselves in the 20th!"

A quarter-of-a-century earlier, F. J. Harvey Darton visited Affpuddle, Bryantspuddle, and Turnerspuddle and found the last to be "the most exquisite" of the trio.

Referring to the de Toneres family, he writes: "They rendered service to the crown of Edward I, and that is about all their history. If their lives were as retired and obscure as their record, they can have chosen no more satisfying a place of retreat than this tiny hamlet.

74

Was this the Turnerspuddle Parsonage, described by Hutchins as "a mean cottage, chiefly built of mud"?

Today it consists of a little gracious farmhouse, two or three cottages, and a toy church, so small and compact and neat that it should hardly be more than a cathedral for Lilliput. Small though it is, it yet contains a Norman font—a last relic of departed strength.

"There is," he goes on "no Norman air about Toner's Piddle. It is just a little farm set in rich deep water meadows below the huge brown heath which breaks out immediately behind the barton. It is in a place of streams, a maze of fords and footbridges: bright with yellow iris and meadowsweet, willow-herb and loosestrife, a haunt of moorhens and herons."

In the 18th and 19th centuries, the picture was not dissimilar. Hutchins' *History . . . of Dorset* records that, in 1790, the houses numbered nineteen and the population ninety-four. Most inhabitants were farm labourers and the women supplemented their incomes in the winter months by buttoning, knitting, and reed-drawing, for the last of which they were paid by the 100 bundles.

"There are four acres of glebe in which stands the parsonage, a mean cottage, chiefly built of mud, and tenanted by two poor families; also a tolerably roomy barn, built of mud," reports the third edition of Hutchins, published in the 1860s.

75

Turnerspuddle was, then as now, something of a backwater, utterly rural in nature and relatively remote from the more civilized parts of England and the rapid advances of the industrial revolution. It and villages like it were steeped in the traditions of their area, their inhabitants well-schooled in country customs and not unsusceptible to superstitions. Nearby was the mysterious wilderness of Thomas Hardy's Egdon Heath, which he was later to describe so vividly in the opening pages of *The Return of the Native.* It was a character in this same novel, Susan Nunsuch, who created a wax image of Eustacia Yeobright prior to casting an evil spell upon her intended victim. Then there "came from between her lips a murmur of words. It was a strange jargon—the Lord's Prayer repeated backwards—the incantation usual in proceedings for obtaining unhallowed assistance against an enemy. Susan uttered the lugubrious discourse three times slowly . . . "

In another scene, Susan follows Eustacia—the "witch-lady" of Egdon Heath—to church, intent on effecting the traditional remedy for being overlooked by a witch—blood-letting.

" . . . a most terrible screech sounded through the church, as if somebody had just gied up their heart's blood. All the folks jumped up, and then we found that Susan Nunsuch had pricked Miss Vye with a long stocking-needle, as she had threatened to do as soon as ever she could get the young lady to church, where she don't come very often. She've waited for this chance for weeks, so as to draw her blood and put an end to the bewitching of Susan's children that has carried on for so long."

Such incidents were rarely the exclusive products of Hardy's imagination. His knowledge of Wessex folklore and customs was profound and he used it in his novels constantly. There were many real-life Susan Nunsuches and Eustacia Vyes, practising their crafts for good or for evil in a variety of ways for a variety of purposes. The purposes of Thomas Tyher of Charminster, near Dorchester—excommunicated in 1616 for witchcraft—were plain enough, at least in the eyes of churchwarden John Foxly.

"I present the said Tyher," Foxly wrote, "for using unchaste means with many women and maids, making them believe that he cannot help them without either crossing their foreskins or lying with them, and many other such unlawful and indirect means the said Tyher doth practise."

Tyher was also accused of "giving purgations unto those that be with child and unmarried, as harlots and suchlike"; of "saying that Joane Blick of Charminster had seven devils in her and for undertaking to cast them out of her"; and of "ministering physic" and publicly using "the casting of waters without knowledge and authority".

The motives of John Walsh of Netherbury, near Beaminster, examined in 1566 for activities "touching witchcraft and sorcery", may have been more honourable, his declared aim being the practice of "physic and surgery". Walsh was persuaded to reveal some of the secrets of his "art", which included the expert advice of fairies whom he met on prehistoric burial mounds. He also spoke of a book inherited from his late master, which had "great circles in it", and of a ritual involving two candles of virgin wax, laid to form a cross within a circle, plus a little frankincense.

Joan Guppy, of South Perrot, on the Dorset-Somerset border, sought the protection of the law in 1604 after she was ambushed on her way to market by several people who suspected her of bewitching Margaret Abington, who had been ill for three years. The attackers, armed with staves, swords, daggers and "other warlike weapons", thrust pins into Joan Guppy's body and tore her face with brambles, saying she was a witch and they had come for her blood and would have it and her life also before they left. Other villagers took Guppy's side, signing a petition declaring not only that they had not known her to indulge in witchcraft or sorcery but that she had done good to many people, curing their wounds "and such like things".

Under Acts of 1541 and 1603, witchcraft was punishable by death and the penalty was not abolished until 1735. Even then, superstition and belief in the supernatural arts remained widespread, especially in country areas. It is not difficult to imagine that such beliefs would have survived, perhaps even flourished, in the lower Piddle Valley. It was at Turnerspuddle, in 1774, that the parish priest recorded the baptism and subsequent burial of twins Joseph and Mary Woodrow, born deformed in early November and interred on the 21st and 27th of that month respectively. The Rev. Samuel Milborne's description of the deformities, and of the suspected reason for them, is perhaps, a further indication of the superstitious nature of his parishioners.

"The above twins when born," he wrote, "had no upper-lip, no upper-jaw, no roof to their mouth, but had a piece of flesh which came from the uvula to the nostrils and hung down from them in such a manner as to form a resemblance as near as possible to a pig's nose, when it closed with the under-lip, to which there was joined another piece of flesh that made the resemblance the more strong: occasioned, as was supposed, from a fright the mother received by drawing a pig from a well."

It was against this backdrop of superstition and rustication that in 1787, following the death of Samuel Milborne in the previous year, the

Rev. William Ettrick arrived to take over as vicar of Affpuddle and rector of Turnerspuddle. He was a young and intelligent minister, well-educated and not, at least in his own view, of a gullible nature. Witchcraft was not a phenomenon in which he believed.

By the time he left the parish many years later, however, he was of a very different mind.

The person responsible for this reversal of opinion was one Susan Woodrow, who came to work for the Ettricks in February 1804. At that time Britain was at war with Napoleon and a French invasion was feared. Almost everywhere, preparations for the defence of the nation were in evidence. Signal stations had been set up along the coast, eight of them in Dorset, and, inland, beacons stood ready to light up the sky in the event of a landing by the enemy. Supply depots had also been established around the county and troops made ready to counter any invasion. The preparations were extraordinarily thorough, including as they did not only a census of Dorset's human population but of the livestock and food stocks too, and plans for their movement if the worst came to pass.

At Turnerspuddle, though, there was a new mood of optimism in the Ettrick household following the arrival in mid-February of Susan Woodrow. For the wage of a shilling a day, she was employed to work in the garden, for which she was reputed to have a particular talent. No one welcomed her arrival more than the Rev. Ettrick himself, for gardening was not his forte.

"Attempting garden work myself two weeks ago," he noted in his diary on February 23, "I have been ill for a long while in sore throat and cold as usual on such occasions. We were therefore rejoiced at hearing of her powers in that way, and give her all encouragement."

Within four days, however, Ettrick's rejoicing had turned to concern, for the horse on which he relied to carry him around his scattered parish had "caught a bad illness". Ettrick blamed the cold weather and the fact that the horse had been "kept too long without moving about" and he gave it "a drench of gin and warm ale to ease the pain in his bowels and make him stale". The remedy proved ineffective and the next day Ettrick sent for John Alder the farrier to give "a drench of my own preparing, which we could not get into him by ourselves". They also removed from the horse a quart of blood, which "relieved him much by next day, and then Alder put down two balls of soap and reub and nitre of my own preparing. He charged only 1s. 6d. for his pains for all, alleging that we kept him well on rammel cheese and good ale."

The horse's ill health was followed by other misfortunes. On April

16, Ettrick recorded the failure of his grass seed and on June 6 wrote that the higher garden was "still unplanted with potatoes" as a consequence of Susan Woodrow being "long time hindered by sickness". She was back now, though, and had finished setting the potatoes in the higher garden by June 13.

In July, Ettrick wrote that his horse had cut his forefoot, causing a lameness that was to last more than three weeks. A lotion was applied and a bandage tied around the leg. In the house, though, there was cause for celebration, for on July 22, Elizabeth Ettrick gave birth to their fourth child, a boy. The birth was attended by five women, including Susan Woodrow, who acted as nurse.

On August 20, Ettrick noted that Susan Woodrow was busy reaping the garden peas, assisted occasionally by himself and a female called Martha.

On August 26, he wrote: "Six gallons of vinegar made, but was not quite so sour as it should have been."

Worse was to come. At the beginning of September, "the poor old horse" caught a cold and "the strangles" to a violent degree. John Alder was called in again and set about bleeding the beast and giving him "some poisonous Hotchpotch ointment". He predicted that the ointment would relieve the suffering creature but in the event it "put him into great anguish". Within twenty-four hours it was clear that the ointment had blistered the horse's throat. He was, wrote his owner, very ill and entirely off his appetite. Alder's poison had created an additional disease on his chest and his lungs were ruined. Alder arrived once more on September 3 to help give another drench or cooling purge and to put a rowel—a small wheel with points on a spur—in the horse's chest. He came again that evening to turn the rowel and the cleryman reported: "The horse seemed something better, but yet cannot eat. Gave the decoction of the same senna and aniseed."

Ten days later, the horse was still very ill. Ettrick was beginning to doubt John Alder's veterinary skills and Alder himself failed to keep his latest appointment. The rector's fears were confirmed when he met a second farrier, Charles Way, and described the treatments Alder had been administering. Way "laughed at the old fellow's methods and poisonous remedy", which had served only to create "other alarming collections of humours about the chest, without relieving the throat".

The following day, both Way and Alder arrived at the rector's stable and Ettrick informed the latter that his services were no longer required. He asked Way to take over and the new man rubbed ointment on to the horse's chest and began other forms of treatment. His efforts continued for two days, but the horse's condition deteriorated further until, on September 16, Ettrick recorded sadly: "The horse has dragged on a painful existence till 8 o'clock this morning, when he fell and expired in one sight after drinking some warmed water rather eagerly."

If the Rev. William Ettrick expected a reversal of fortunes at this juncture, he was to be disappointed. On September 22, he noted in his diary that "an ailing pig was killed to prevent it dying, and was salted for food".

The rector of Turnerspuddle and vicar of Affpuddle was beginning to wonder if he really was just the victim of bad luck or whether there were other forces at work. On October 3, he wrote: "Walked over to Dairyman Oliver's to bespeak two pigs, intending to kill the fat one in a few days more, Deo volente, if he be not cut off by witchcraft of our notorious neighbours before that time."

This witchcraft, he went on, was now believed by the family to be responsible not only for the horse's lameness, long illness, and eventual death but also for the loss of their dog, the sickness of the pig which had had to be slaughtered, and the "intolerable plague and tormenting" of their young children. The youngest child had required almost constant nursing since he was born in July. The poor mite was suffering from a "peculiar and most vexatious illness", which occupied "the whole time of some one person all the hours of the day, even when in the cradle, but at night still doubly so, the rage commencing just at the time when we should go to repose and the child obliged to be kept in arms first by one and then another, all the night, by turns".

William Ettrick was now utterly convinced about the cause of his family's catalogue of recent misfortune. He likened the condition of his youngest child to a "demonical possession", which had begun "immediately after the child was snatched out of the mother's arms, by a hag and reputed witch". To counter the witch's work, the country clergyman tied a phylactery or charm, inscribed with sacred words, around the baby's body. The remedy had an immediate and "wonderful" result, bringing about a "sudden and entire peace, and healthy symptoms in all respects"—effects that, he claimed, no medical remedy could ever obtain.

"I was once," he declared on November 14, "incredulous about the power of witchcraft, but have no doubts remaining."

He was even convinced that a horse he had twice borrowed from Mrs Alner to fetch a cartload of potatoes from Affpuddle had become a target for the same "vile witchcraft of a bad neighbour", for the beast had become "very weak and seemingly going the way of mine".

On November 26, Ettrick paid John Alder's bill for blacksmithing

The tiny church of Turnerspuddle, now disused.

work and "relieved him of the blame of killing the horse", saying that he "attributed it to an evil influence" and telling "how the child had been affected and how cured by application of certain means".

The baby's recovery from his agonizing illness coincided with the absence from the household for two weeks of Susan Woodrow. But towards the end of November, she returned to the clergyman's employ to do washing and other work. Almost immediately, the child began to suffer a relapse. For the Rev. William Ettrick, it was far more than coincidence.

"We have reasons very strong and many to ascribe to this ill-looking and worse-tempered wretch: the sufferings of this child, the curse upon the horse, etc.," he wrote on December 1. "She has often dropped expressions that excite great suspicion and express pleasure (at) trouble, saying it was right, and as it should be, with a malignant grin, but never once offered the bare civility of wishing the child better, which is most surprising, so much as we have befriended her."

The diary entry added: "While her connections with the house remain, we shall remain under power, and are come to a determine to dismiss her."

Despite his declared resolve, Ettrick delayed the dismissal for several weeks, perhaps fearing the consequences of such an act. Then, at the beginning of January 1805, he had a powerful dream, which seems finally to have convinced him that it was time to act.

"I dreamed that an ill-omened black-looking bird with strange outcries, after flying round the parlour where I was sitting, several times pitched upon my head on the crown of my hat," he wrote. "I presently seized it and, taking it to the door, wrung its neck about, yet not without some difficulty from it hideous cries and attempts to hurt me. The cat being in sight, eyed the bird with avidity at first, but on seeing it thrown on the ground, would not approach it, though killed."

Ettrick interpreted the dream as an accurate reflection of his family's experiences with Susan Woodrow. It expressed, he concluded, "her power, long triumph, close fixing on us and reluctance to yield her diabolical influence", followed by "our final victory and the truth of our suspicions of what she was—not meat even for a cat."

Three days later, on January 4, 1805, Ettrick gave Susan Woodrow a "sharp and final discharge from ever being employed by me any more". She was, he noted, a good all-round worker whose qualities in this respect easily compensated for her "lying and uncommon impudence". But she was also a woman of "hollowness and deceit", traits which "too much obstructed the benefit" of her work around the house and garden.

"We have now," the rector added, "traced home to her, in a manner that sets all doubt at defiance, the whole of the miseries and misfortunes that have fallen so thick and heavy on us and our affairs ever since her engagement."

Susan Woodrow was reluctant to accept her dismissal and returned later the same day with two letters and an intention to "worm herself into our good opinion and regain our work". She asked repeatedly what she had done, but Ettrick refused to answer her or to receive the letters and threatened to obtain a warrant if she did not leave immediately.

Ettrick's diary goes on to describe in great and repetitive detail what he calls the "works of Susan" and their consequences—a "continued series of disastrous events of all things attempted by us of which she had any knowledge or participation in". These included not only the various afflictions of the children and the losses of the dog, pig, and the "hard and healthy and not very old horse" but also various horticultural disasters, such as the rotting of the best potatoes sorted and stored by Susan while lesser specimens dealt with by others remained in good condition.

"Sue took a great offence while doing this job and punishes us with a loss of about £3 hereby, as potatoes sell now at 12s. a bag," he observed.

Other failures in the garden included the broad clover and sainfoin, sown in the mid-garden and yielding not a single plant, the savoys and parsnips, which fared no better, and also the raspberries and "most of the gardening done by her at 2s. a day and drink". Such losses were, of course, far more significant in 1804 than they would be today, for then the English cottage garden played no mean role in sustaining the rural population.

Ettrick also described an incident that the took to be a "very remarkable proof against Sue", which had occurred not long before the horse first fell ill.

"On my trimming the mane and tail of the mare," he recalled, "Sue begged I would give her a small part of the hair pulled out to make up a pound for her son to sell to Mr J. Shave, the saddler, as he had part but not enough to make weight. I said she was welcome to it all, that I had no use for it. But she picked up a few locks, saying, 'That will do, that will do', in answer to my renewed offers of the whole. And so it did, being a free gift from me, and only wanted for the purpose of bewitching my beast to death and not to sell. From that time the illness began, and baffled all remedy, although of easy cure generally."

Ettrick had further discovered that the livestock of Susan Woodrow's previous employer, Thomas Saunders, had suffered in a similar manner to his own. Saunders' horse was "drooping for many weeks" before "dying without ostensible cause"—an event which Woodrow subsequently related "with singular glee". This was not the only loss sustained by Saunders during that year, the others including five calves out of eight, "it being uncommon to lose any". By way of further evidence, the diary refers to "Susan's pain at the heart or left side at that time, occasioned by some methods used by Thomas or Joseph Saunders, who also had many losses and was equally hated by her".

Was Susan Woodrow really a witch, as the Rev. William Ettrick believed? Or was the country clergyman so desperate to find an explanation for the misfortunes that befell his family that he was prepared to compromise his own scepticism and apply the gossip and superstition of his parishioners to his own situation? We are, of course, not only unable to discover what Susan Woodrow felt about the matter but almost wholly dependent on Ettrick's own interpretation of events as set down over a twenty-month period in his diary. Even that is incomplete, for the original diary appears to have been lost long since, leaving us with only a typescript copy of extracts.

One factor that might lend weight to his conviction would be evidence of motive. The diary extracts offer little in this respect, though an entry dated October 3, 1804, does provide a hint by suggesting that the latest "persecutions originate from the poor horse getting into their grass, without our knowledge, the fences being down". And the entry of January 4, 1805, refers to "the motive—partly malice natural to a witch and partly interest—nothing to be done without victuals and pay constantly for Susan".

What is certain is that Ettrick confidently expected events in his household to take a turn for the better following the departure of Susan Woodrow in January 1805. He received some encouragement on March 11, when a pig-killing was performed "as usual with eclat" by William Clarke.

"It turned out better than expectation, having not thriven well during the administration of the Witch Susan, who had been deterred from very active mischief by my threats against the witch unknown who killed the former one. Everything partook of a share of her blessing, and all begins to go on as well heretofore in proportion as we publish her character the more."

The following month, however, he was talking pessimistically about the expected fortunes of the latest attempt at home-made vinegar, observing that "we never had a black cat till she came and now have had two in succession, though none such is in this neighbourhood".

The final diary entry of which we are aware, dated September 11, 1805, refers to the family's stock of bees having "dwindled away unaccountably, Susan having had hands upon them last year."

"They have not swarmed once this year, though some were very heavy and two have declined and gone, leaving empty combs. Keep no more bees," the entry adds.

Whether Susan Woodrow and her magical powers continued to blight the Ettrick family of Turnerspuddle, or whether they believed that she did so, we will probably never know. Nor do we know whether her reputed activities played any part in Ettrick's decision to resign his post and leave the parish, as he did just three years later in 1808.

What became of Susan Woodrow we are also unsure, but there is no evidence to suggest that any harm befell her. Was she, perhaps, the Susannah Woodrow who outlived most of her contemporaries and whose burial at the grand age of eighty was recorded by one of Ettrick's successors in the Turnerspuddle parish register on May 6, 1838? We cannot be sure.

7

The Grave of the Ripper?
The mystery of M. J. Druitt and the Whitechapel murders of 1888

On January 3, 1889, members of one of Wimborne's most respected and respectable families gathered to pay their last respects to one of their loved ones. It was, as the *Dorset County Chronicle and Somersetshire Gazette* reported, a sad occasion; and it followed what the same paper euphemistically described as a "distressing occurrence" in the River Thames at Chiswick. The body of Montague John Druitt was recovered from the river at noon on the last day of 1888. His coat had been weighted with stones and it appeared he had been in the water for about a month. He had left a note alluding to suicide and a second note stating that "Since Friday I have felt as if I was going to be like mother"—presumed to be a reference to the mental illness from which his mother had been suffering for several months. Druitt, who was thirty-one, had drowned and an inquest jury returned a verdict that he committed suicide "while of unsound mind".

Druitt was buried in Wimborne cemetery in a grave adjacent to the plot occupied by the remains of his father, William Druitt, a surgeon and a Justice of the Peace. A memorial stone was erected bearing the simple inscription "In memory of Mon. Jno. Druitt, Dec. 4, 1888". There was, of course, no mention of the cause of Druitt's death; and there was certainly no mention of the suspicion that his family are said to have held that they may have been interring the corpse of Jack the Ripper. More than six-and-a-half decades were to pass before these suspicions were publicly revealed.

Jack the Ripper was the most notorious killer of his generation and one of the most infamous of all time. In the space of a few months in 1888, he ended the lives of five prostitutes (some have claimed there were seven or even more victims but five is now the generally accepted number) and sent tidal waves of terror around the East End of London and shock waves throughout the country. It was not just the fact of the

Druitt's gravestone in Wimborne Cemetery. *(Photo: Evening Echo, Bournemouth)*

killings that sent the population into panic but the manner of them, the horrific mutilations they involved.

The Ripper's first undisputed victim, Mary Ann Nichols, was found dead in Buck's Row (now Dorset Street), Whitechapel, at 3.40 a.m. on Friday August 31, 1888. She was lying on her back, eyes open, clothes pushed up above her knees. Her throat had been cut from ear to ear, severing her windpipe, gullet, and spinal cord, and she had also been disembowelled. Other injuries included two stab wounds to the genitals and bruising to the right side of the jaw that could have been caused by the pressure of gripping fingers.

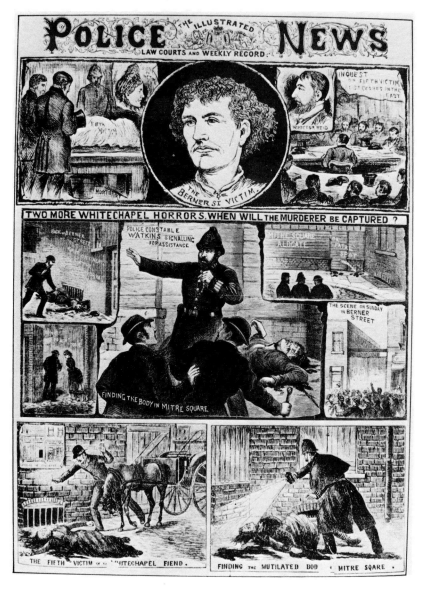

The murders of Stride and Eddowes make front page news.

Victim number two died eight days later, in the early hours of September 8, in the backyard of 29 Hanbury Street less than a mile from Buck's Row. She was identified as Annie Chapman, also known as Dark Annie and Annie Siffey or Sievey. Like Nichols, she lay on her back, knees wide apart, skirt pushed up, face bruised and swollen, neck deeply and jaggedly cut from the left. Like Nichols, she had been disembowelled. Her stomach had been torn open, sections of skin and intestine had been placed on her shoulders, and her bladder, uterus, and part of her vagina had been cut out and taken away. Her rings had been torn from her fingers and nearby lay some pennies and two farthings that had probably come from her clothing.

It was about 1 a.m. on September 30, a wet and windy night, when Swedish-born Elizabeth Stride, known as Long Liz, met her end in a yard in Berner Street. Her throat had been slit from left to right, but there were no other mutilations and her body was still warm when found. She had been seen alive and well just fifteen minutes earlier and the evidence suggested that the noise of the finder's pony and trap had disturbed the killer before his work was through.

He did not have to wait long to find another victim, however. At the very time that he was making his getaway from Berner Street, another prostitute, Catherine Eddowes, was taking her leave from Bishopsgate police station after an evening in custody for being drunk and disorderly. Forty-five minutes later, patrolling PC Watkins found her body in Mitre Square. In his words, the victim had been ripped open "like a pig in a market". Her throat had been slit, her face slashed, and part of her nose and right ear had been sliced off. Like Mary Nichols and Annie Chapman, she had been disembowelled and her uterus and left kidney had been taken away.

Forty days passed before the fifth and final murder and it differed from the others in several ways. At twenty-five, Mary Jane Kelly was by far the youngest of the Ripper's victims; she was also more attractive and, unlike the others, she was killed indoors; and the mutilations carried out on her body were appalling even by the killer's own horrific standards. The *Illustrated Police News* reported: "The throat had been cut right across with a knife, nearly severing the head from the body. The abdomen had been partially ripped open, and both of the breasts had been cut from the body. The left arm, like the head, hung to the body by the skin only. The nose had been cut off, the forehead skinned, and the thighs, down to the feet, stripped of the flesh. The abdomen had been slashed with a knife across downwards, and the liver and entrails wrenched away. The entrails and other portions of the frame were missing but the liver etc., it is said, were found placed between the feet of the poor victim. The flesh from the thighs and legs, together with the breasts and nose, had been placed by the murderer on the table, and one of the hands of the dead woman had been pushed in her stomach."

Mary Kelly's body was found on November 9 in her rented room at Miller's Court off Dorset Street. A few feet from the centre of the carnage lay her clothes, neatly folded on a chair. In the grate were warm ashes from a fierce fire in which a woman's clothing had been burned. Whose clothing it was—for it was not Mary Kelly's, apparently—and why it was burned remains one of the lesser puzzles within the greater Ripper riddle.

Long before the Kelly killing, public excitement over the murders had reached fever pitch. Mobs moved about the streets of London until nightfall or gathered outside police stations chanting "Murderer" at anyone unlucky enough to have been arrested, in many cases for some trivial offence. Enterprising neighbours of Annie Chapman charged visiting ghouls a few pence a time to gaze on the yard where she died. The newspapers helped to whip up hysteria with their sensational reporting of the killings and their attacks on the police for failing to bring the killer to justice.

There were clues—some genuine, some red herrings—for the police to follow up. A leather apron found near Annie Chapman's body threw suspicion on a boot finisher known to wear such a garment in connection with his work but he was released after two days' questioning. Four of the five victims were seen talking to men near the scenes of their deaths, in two cases less than fifteen minutes before their bodies were found. Mary Kelly was seen arriving at Miller's Court twice in less than three hours on the night of her death, each time with a man in tow. And between 3.30 and 4 a.m. two people heard a cry of "Murder!" but thought little of it. After the Mitre Square murder, the killer dropped a piece of bloodstained material from his victim's apron some distance away in Goulston Street. Chalked on a wall nearby was a cryptic message, which most have assumed had been left by the Ripper. "The Juwes are The men That Will not be Blamed for nothing," it said. Surprisingly, the message was erased by order of the Metropolitan Police Commissioner, Sir Charles Warren, before it could be photographed, on the grounds that it might inflame prejudice against the local Jewish community.

The most significant clues of all—or perhaps the biggest red herrings—were a letter and a postcard written in boastful, taunting terms, signed by Jack the Ripper (it was these communications that gave the killer his famous name) and sent to the Central News Agency

The killing of Mary Kelly as depicted by the *Penny Illustrated Paper*.

bearing the postmarks September 27 and October 1 respectively. The letter included mockery of the police attempts to catch him, a statement that he was "down on whores and I shan't quit ripping them till I do get bucked", and a warning that "the next job I do I shall clip the lady's ears off and send to the police officers just for jolly". The postcard said: "I was not codding dear old Boss when I gave you the tip. You'll hear about Saucy Jack's work tomorrow. Double event this time. Number one squealed a bit. Couldn't finish straight off. Had not time to get ears for police. Thanks for keeping last letter back till I got to work again."

The case for the authenticity of the correspondence is convincing since, although details of the "double event" appeared in the papers on October 1, the existence of the first letter (which included a request for it to be kept back) was not made public until October 2, the day after the second postmark.

Over the years, many candidates have been proposed for the title of Jack the Ripper. One view, widely held since the time of the killings, is that the Ripper was a medical man or at least someone with more than a passing knowledge of anatomy. This view was fuelled not only by the black medical-type bag carried by someone acting suspiciously a few hours after the Miller's Court murder but by the comments of doctors who carried out post-mortem examinations on the victims. The mutilations perpetrated on the body of Mary Nichols were said to have been "deftly and skilfully performed" while those on Annie Chapman were "obviously the work of an expert—or one, at least, who had such knowledge of anatomical or pathological examinations as to be enabled to secure the pelvic organs with one sweep of the knife". The treatment of Catherine Eddowes convinced one doctor that the killer was "no stranger to the knife", a second that he "possessed some anatomical knowledge", and a third that he had only the kind of knowledge one would expect of a butcher. The only comment on the extreme mutilations on Kelly, however, was that they indicated "no scientific or anatomical knowledge".

Some Victorian detectives are said to have been convinced that the Ripper was a mad Russian doctor. Several East Europeans have been nominated, including Polish-born barber-surgeon George Chapman (formerly Severin Antoniovitch Klosowski), hanged in 1903 after poisoning three women. Another multiple poisoner, Dr Thomas Neill Cream, who included London prostitutes among his victims, joined the contenders for the Ripper title in 1892 when his hangman heard him utter the words "I was Jack the ——" before dying with the sentence unfinished. So did a Harley Street surgeon called Dr Stanley in 1929 when Leonard Matters, an Australian journalist, cleverly wove a mixture of fact and fantasy into a book which claimed that his fictitiously-named subject had avenged the ruination of his son's life by a syphilitic prostitute. A plausible case has even been made out to support the contention that Jack the Ripper was really Jill the Ripper, a midwife or female abortionist.

Some candidates have been eminent and highly respectable members of the community, such as James Monro, who became Commissioner of the Metropolitan Police in December 1888. In recent years there have also been several theories directly or indirectly linking the royal family to the murders. The first of these was put forward in an article in *The Criminologist* magazine in 1970 by Dr Thomas Stowell, an elderly surgeon who described the Ripper as "an heir to power and wealth" whose "family had for 50 years earned the love and admiration of large numbers of people by its devotion to public service". Stowell named his suspect only as "S" and publicly denied that he was referring to Queen Victoria's grandson, Albert Victor, Duke of Clarence, also known as Prince Eddy, who was second in line to the throne until his early death in 1892. Privately, however, he admitted that Clarence was his man—and that he had reached this conclusion after examining in the 1930s the papers of the royal physician, Sir William Gull. These apparently revealed that Clarence had not died in a 'flu epidemic, as claimed by the history books, but in a mental home near Sandringham of softening of the brain due to syphilis. They also linked him with the Cleveland Street scandal of 1889, suggesting he was one of those questioned about sodomy with telegraph boys, and dropped hints about his involvement in the Ripper murders.

This theory led to another, which proposed that Stowell had misinterpreted Gull's notes and that "S" was not the Duke at all but his friend and former Cambridge tutor, J. K. Stephen. Stephen was certainly known to Gull, who treated him for head injuries sustained in a riding accident in 1886. The patient appeared to make a full recovery at first but subsequently became strangely lethargic and increasingly odd in his behaviour before eventually going to a mental home for two years before his death in 1892. He was also a woman hater and wrote poems in which women were reviled.

Close on the heels of the Clarence and Stephen theories came another set of startling revelations from Joseph Sickert, son of the Victorian painter Walter Sickert. Walter had a studio in Cleveland Street, Soho, and it was there, according to Joseph, that he introduced the high-living Duke of Clarence to a shop girl who modelled for him, Annie Elizabeth Crook. The pair become lovers and in 1885 Annie gave birth to the Duke's child, Alice Margaret. Soon afterwards, the prince and the shopgirl married in a private ceremony witnessed by Sickert and the baby's nanny, Marie Jeannette Kelly. The news leaked back to the Palace and the Prime Minister and a plan was hatched to remove the risk of a scandal. Annie was certified insane and confined in a mental institution and her daughter was cared for by Kelly. Alice eventually found her way back to Sickert and grew up to become his mistress and the mother of Joseph. According to Joseph, Kelly told the story to some of her prostitute friends and decided to blackmail the royal family. Sir William Gull was given the task of eliminating the blackmailers—Kelly, Nichols, Chapman, and Stride—but also happened to kill Eddowes by mistake (she was also known as Mary Ann Kelly).

The Sickert story was first told publicly on BBC television in 1973 but a young journalist, Stephen Knight, took it a step or two further and alleged in a book that the killings were carried out according to Masonic ritual by a three-strong team which included not only Gull but Walter Sickert himself.

It was on another television programme some years earlier that Montague John Druitt was first publicly identified as a Jack the Ripper candidate, though at that stage only by his initials, M. J. D.

Druitt was born at Wimborne on August 15 1857, one of seven children fathered by the town's leading surgeon, William Druitt. At the age of thirteen, he won a scholarship to Winchester College, where he played an active role in drama, debating, and sport. His thespian talents were dubious (a critic wrote in the college magazine that his Toby Belch in *Twelfth Night* was "better imagined than described"), but he shone in debating and excelled at rugby and cricket, becoming the school fives champion and playing at Lords in 1876 as a member of the college first eleven. In his final year at Winchester, he was elected prefect of the chapel and also won another scholarship, to New College, Oxford.

Druitt's sporting talents were quickly recognized at Oxford and in the freshman's match of 1877 he took five wickets for thirty for the New College eleven in the second innings. He also represented the college at rugger and was the university fives champion in 1877. Academically, Druitt was somewhat less successful, managing only a third-class honours degree in classics when he graduated in 1880.

The surgeon's son chose a career in law, but two years passed before he was admitted to the Inner Temple. His studies were financed partly by loans from his father, the money to be deducted from a £500 legacy that William Druitt had already set aside for him. Montague was called

93

to the Bar in March 1885. The same year his father died, leaving an estate worth £16,579 to be divided between Montague's mother, elder brother, and three sisters, with little provision for the three younger sons.

Soon after qualifying as a barrister, Druitt rented chambers at 9 Kings Bench Walk and joined the Western Circuit. It was, however, a difficult period for barristers—it was reckoned that only one in eight could make a living at his chosen profession—and it appears that in his three years at the Bar, Druitt failed to attract a single brief. In the meantime, he continued to work—as he had done since 1881—as a teacher at Blackheath private boys' school, for whom he was also able to play cricket against many reputable sides, including the MCC.

At the end of the Michaelmas term 1888, Druitt's life took a further turn for the worse when he was sacked by the head of Blackheath, George Valentine. The reason for his dismissal is not known. It has been suggested that homosexuality was behind it but there is no real evidence to support this. Perhaps Druitt's own deteriorating state of mind was a major factor. He could not have been happy about his failure to make his way as a barrister and since July 1888 his mother had been confined in a private asylum for the insane. Now, apparently, he feared a similar fate for himself.

Montague Druitt was last seen alive on Monday December 3, 1888. On December 11, his elder brother, William, a solicitor living in Bournemouth, learned that Montague had been missing from his chambers for more than a week. William travelled to London to make inquiries and heard for the first time about his brother's dismissal. He searched his things and found a note addressed to himself.

Druitt's body was discovered in the Thames near Thorneycroft's torpedo works at Chiswick on December 31 by a waterman named Winslow or Winslade. Two days later, an inquest was held at the Lamb Tap in Church Street, Chiswick, and on January 5 the proceedings were reported in the *Acton, Chiswick and Turnham Green Gazette* under the headline "Found Drowned":

"William H. Druitt said that he lived at Bournemouth and that he was a solicitor. The deceased was his brother, who was 31 last birthday. He was a barrister-at-law and an assistant master in a school at Blackheath. He had stayed with witness at Bournemouth for a night towards the end of October. Witness heard from a friend on the 11th of December that deceased had not been heard of at his chambers for more than a week. Witness had deceased's things searched where he resided and found a paper addressed to him (produced). The Coroner read the letter, which was to this effect: 'Since Friday I felt I was going

94

to be like mother and the best thing for me was to die.'"

William Druitt told the inquest that his brother had never made any attempt on his life before and that his mother had become insane in the previous July. He added that he had no other relative—a curious statement for a member of a reasonably large family.

The report went on: "Henry Winslade was the next witness. He said he lived at No. 4, Shore Street, Paxton Road, and that he was a waterman. About one o'clock on Monday he was on the river in a boat when he saw the body floating. The tide was at half flood, running up. He brought the body ashore and gave information to the police.

"PC George Moulson 216T said he searched the body which was fully dressed excepting the hat and collar. He found four large stones in each pocket in the top coat; £2 10s. in gold, 7s. in silver, 2d. in bronze, two cheques on the London and Provincial Bank (one for £50 and the other for £16), a first-class season pass from Blackheath to London (South Western Region), a second half return Hammersmith to Charing Cross (dated 1st December), a silver watch, gold chain with a spade guinea attached, a pair of kid gloves and a white handkerchief. There were no papers or letters of any kind. There were no marks of injury to the body but it was rather decomposed."

The newspaper added: "A verdict of suicide whilst in an unsound state of mind was returned."

The "Druitt for Ripper" theory owes much to the writings of Sir Melville Macnaghten, who was appointed Assistant Chief Constable at Scotland Yard in June 1889 and head of CID in 1903. In his memoirs, published in 1914, he expressed his regret that he became a detective officer "six months after the so-called 'Jack the Ripper' committed suicide" and consequently "never had a go at that fascinating individual".

Some years earlier, in February 1894, Macnaghten produced seven foolscap pages of handwritten notes in response to a "sensational story" in "The Sun" newspaper in which a certain Thomas Cutbush was denounced as Jack the Ripper. Cutbush had appeared at the London County Sessions charged with maliciously wounding one woman and attempting to wound another; he had been declared insane and sentenced to be detained during Her Majesty's Pleasure. In defence of Cutbush, whose offences were minor by comparison, Macnaghten observed that in the Ripper murders "the fury of the mutilations increased in each case, and, seemingly, the appetite only became sharpened by indulgence".

He went on: "It seems, then, highly improbable that the murderer would have suddenly stopped in November '88, and been content to recommence operations by merely prodding a girl's behind some two years and four months afterwards. A much more rational theory is that the murderer's brain gave way altogether after his awful glut in Miller's Court, and that he immediately committed suicide, or, as a possible alternative, was found to be so hopelessly mad by his relations, that he was by them confined in some asylum."

The notes then name three suspects, any one of whom, says Macnaghten, would have been more likely than Cutbush to have committed the Ripper crimes. The first was "a Mr M. J. Druitt, said to be a doctor and of good family—who disappeared at the time of the Miller's Court murder, and whose body (which was said to have been upwards of a month in the water) was found in the Thames on 31st December— or about seven weeks after that murder. He was sexually insane and from private information I have little doubt but that his own family believed him to have been the murderer."

The second named suspect was Kosminski, "a Polish Jew and resident in Whitechapel. This man became insane owing to many years indulgence in solitary vices. He had a great hatred of women, specially of the prostitute class, and had strong homicidal tendencies: he was removed to a lunatic asylum about March 1889. There were many circumstances connected with this man which made him a strong 'suspect.'"

The third was Michael Ostrog, "a Russian doctor, and a convict, who was subsequently detained in a lunatic asylum as a homicidal maniac. This man's antecedents were of the worst possible type, and his whereabouts at the time of the murders could never be ascertained."

More than sixty-five years elapsed before the contents of Macnaghten's confidential notes began to seep into the public domain. The first hint of their contents and of Druitt's candidature came in 1959 in a television programme presented by writer and television interviewer Dan Farson following a visit to the North Wales home of Lady Rose McLaren. Lady Rose, the daughter-in-law of the Dowager Lady Aberconway, Macnaghten's daughter, showed Farson a typewritten copy of the former CID chief's notes made, apparently, soon after his death. In accordance with Lady Aberconway's wishes, Farson identified Druitt only by his initials M. J. D. He also remembered, however, that after an earlier television series that had included coverage of the Ripper murders, he had received a letter from a Mr Knowles in Australia concerning a document called "The East End Murderer—I Knew Him", written by one Lionel Druitt, Drewett, or Drewery and "printed privately by a Mr Fell of

Dandenong in 1890". As Farson was aware, M. J. Druitt had a cousin called Lionel Druitt who formerly practised on the Whitechapel-City border and later emigrated to Australia. The frustrating thing for Farson was that he no longer had Mr Knowles' letter: along with other material on the Ripper murders, it had vanished from his desk in Television House. Over the next couple of years, Farson invested much time and money in trying to track down the seemingly crucial document, even visiting Dandenong and meeting someone who remembered Lionel Druitt practising as a doctor in nearby Drovin in 1903. But his efforts were in vain, despite the coverage given to his search by Australian television and newspapers.

By the time Farson published his book on the Ripper in 1972, Druitt's identity was well-known to anyone with an interest in the subject, thanks to another book, Tom Cullen's *Autumn of Terror*, published seven years earlier. Cullen relied heavily on the claims that Jack the Ripper had a knowledge of anatomy, suggesting that Druitt would probably have "gained some knowledge of surgery" by watching his father at work. He also drew attention to evidence from other sources that implied that Macnaghten was not the only policeman to suspect Druitt. As early as March 1889, Albert Backert of the Whitechapel Vigilance Committee, concerned at what he saw as police complacency over the Ripper, was sworn to secrecy and told in confidence: "The man in question is dead. He was fished out of the Thames two months ago and it would only cause pain to relatives if we said any more than that."

Subsequently, Assistant Commissioner Basil Thomson said of the Ripper: "This man escaped arrest by committing suicide." And Sir John Moyland, from the Home Office, stated: "The murderer, it is now certain, escaped arrest by committing suicide at the end of 1888."

In 1898, in his book *Mysteries of Police and Crime,* prison inspector and crime historian Major Arthur Griffiths referred to three unnamed suspects, all of them "homicidal lunatics", against whom the police held "very plausible and reasonable grounds of suspicion". Griffiths was obviously referring to the same trio as Macnaghten, for he identifies one as a Polish Jew who frequented the Whitechapel district and ended up in a lunatic asylum and the second as an insane Russian doctor who habitually carried surgical knives and instruments on his person.

"The third person," Griffiths continued, "was of the same type, but the suspicion in his case was the stronger and there was every reason to believe that his own friends entertained grave doubts about him. He was also a doctor in the prime of his life, was believed to be insane, or

97

on the borderline of insanity, and he disappeared immediately after the last murder, that in Miller's Court on the 9th of November, 1888. On the last day of that year, seven weeks later, his body was found floating in the Thames and was said to have been in the water a month. The theory in this case was that after his last exploit, which was the most fiendish of all, his brain gave way and he became furiously insane and committed suicide."

Since his arrival in the Ripper arena, Montague Druitt's candidature has been examined by many Ripperologists who have reached a variety of conclusions. Donald McCormick asserted that at the times that Mary Ann Nichols and Annie Chapman were murdered, Druitt was not even in London but living in Bournemouth. His source was an unnamed London doctor whose father was at Oxford with the Dorset-born barrister. The doctor further stated that Druitt was being blackmailed by someone who had threatened to denounce him as Jack the Ripper to the school where he worked, that this accounted for the large amount of money found on his body, and that he told his mother of his plight and she in turn informed the police when her son went missing in December 1888.

More definite facts about Druitt's movements in the summer of 1888 appeared in the January 1973 issue of *The Cricketer,* in which Irving Rosenwater looked at his cricketing career. He noted that Druitt was playing at Blackheath on July 21, at Bournemouth on August 3-4 and 10-11, at Canford Magna, near Wimborne, on September 1, and at Blackheath again on September 8. The last two dates are the most significant, since the Canford fixture was played on the day after the Nichols killing, while the second Blackheath match was on the very same day that Chapman died. These facts prove nothing and could be used to support a case against Druitt or to oppose it. Rosenwater chose the former course, pointing out that six hours passed between the time of Chapman's murder and Druitt's appearance on the cricket field at Blackheath. "It was an easy task to make the comparatively short journey from Spitalfields to Blackheath," he wrote, adding that "on the evidence now disclosed, it will require a courageous and learned man to say that the Whitechapel murderer was not Montague John Druitt, cricketer."

Stephen Knight was also unable to dispense with Druitt's involvement in the Ripper affair, but found a different role for him—that of scapegoat. Sickert had claimed this from the beginning, he wrote, and Druitt—"alone in London, nervous and unhappy"—would have been an "ideal choice" for those involved in the cover-up and "questing for a likely candidate on whom to place the blame for the murders." Knight puts forward fourteen connections between Druitt and those involved in the alleged conspiracy. Some are rather tenuous, but one of two may be significant, including the presence in King's Bench Walk (where Druitt had chambers at No. 9) of fellow barristers Harry Lushington Stephen (at No. 3) and Herbert Stephen (opposite No. 9 at 4 Paper Buildings). Both were brothers of Prince Eddy's friend and fellow Ripper suspect J. K. Stephen and all the Stephens were patients of royal surgeon Sir William Gull, yet another suspect. Also based in King's Bench Walk, and actually sharing Druitt's address at No. 9, were fellow lawyers Reginald Brodie Dyke Acland, the brother of Sir William Gull's son-in-law, and Edward Henslow Bedford who, according to Knight, instigated part of the cover-up of the Cleveland Street homosexual brothel scandal of 1889 in which the prince and other society folk were implicated.

"It seems," writes Knight, "beyond coincidence that the man who played a major role in the second part of the cover-up should live at the self-same address as the person used as a scapegoat in the third part. Bedford was in the best possible position to evaluate Druitt, bring him to the notice of those in charge of the cover-up, and also set up his murder."

Knight's picture of Druitt as an innocent scapegoat murdered by society conspirators as part of a cover-up was the third basic conclusion on the Druitt issue to be reached by Ripperologists, the others being that he was Jack the Ripper and that he had nothing to do with the Whitechapel murders whatsoever. An observer might think there were no more variations on the "Druitt for Ripper" theory to be had, but in 1987 Martin Howells and Keith Skinner published a book in which they put forward a fourth contention, namely that Druitt was both the Whitechapel murderer and a murder victim himself.

Central to the Howells-Skinner theory is their assertion that Druitt was a homosexual; this was, they say, the meaning behind Sir Melville Macnaghten's description of him as "sexually insane" and probably also had something to do with his mysterious dismissal from Blackheath boys' school. Even more central is the claim that Druitt was an associate of the sexually deviant Prince Eddy and his clique of Oxbridge graduates.

"If Druitt knew Eddy or any one of his close friends— particularly if this association implied a homosexual liaison—then many unrelated fragments in the Ripper legend would at long last fall into place and the case against Druitt would surely be proven beyond all reasonable doubt," claim Howells and Skinner.

The final assertion may be a rash one, but the writers do offer some

99

LONDON'S REIGN OF TERROR: SCENES OF SUNDAY MORNING'S MURDERS IN THE EAST-END.

More contemporary coverage of the Stride and Eddowes murders.

additional evidence to support the suggestion that Druitt moved in the same circles as Prince Eddy. Scribbled inside the back cover of a diary written by fellow barrister Harry Wilson, one of Eddy's closest friends at Cambridge and after, they found the name J. H. Lonsdale and the address 5 Eliot Cottages, Blackheath. The address was within 100 yards of Blackheath School at 9 Eliot Place, where Druitt taught. Further investigation revealed not only that John Henry Lonsdale too was a barrister but that his chambers were at 4 Kings Bench Walk, next door to H. L. Stephen and five doors from Druitt. H. L. Stephen was also mentioned in the Wilson diary, opposite the words "I love him, I love him". Wilson worked from chambers at the Inns of Court, not far from King's Bench Walk.

"Lonsdale and Druitt lived in sight of each other at Blackheath and they were even closer at the Temple," comment Howells and Skinner. "All the indications were that both men would have known each other well, and at the very least they would have had mutual friends."

Wondering whether there was any end to the coincidences, the authors further discovered that in 1887 Lonsdale gave up his legal career in favour of the Church and that his first ministry was at Wimborne Minster—home town of Montague John Druitt.

Wimborne also provided the next piece of evidence linking Druitt with the highest in the land. From an article in the *Southern Guardian,* we learn that on December 17, 1888, Prince Eddy himself paid an unexpected visit to Dorset, deciding at short notice to join Lord Wimborne's shooting party. A ball was hastily arranged in honour of the royal guest and a guest list drawn up which, to the astonishment of Howells and Skinner, included the names of none other than Montague John Druitt and his mother, Ann Druitt! Lord and Lady Wimborne were not to know that the barrister's weighted body was at that very time lying at the bottom of the Thames. They may or may not have known that his mother was in a mental institution in London. But they would have known that the head of the Druitt family was not Montague but his unmarried brother, William, who lived in Bournemouth, and that he was the proper person to invite with his mother unless there was a specific reason for inviting Montague. Was it simply that the squire of Canford Magna and his lady knew Montague, who had after all played cricket at Canford a few weeks before? Or were they aware that the barrister was a friend of the prince and therefore an appropriate guest for the occasion?

Like so many other elements in the Ripper saga, it is an intriguing possibility. Equally intriguing is the further discovery by Howells and Skinner that at the time of her son's death, Ann Druitt was not at the asylum in Chiswick where she eventually died but at another institution called Brooke, less than two miles northeast of Whitechapel. As Howells and Skinner are eager to point out, she arrived there five weeks before the Ripper killings began and Montague's route from Blackheath to the Brooke asylum would have taken him right through Whitechapel.

Ann's residence at Brooke rather than Chiswick also destroys the previously accepted explanation for Montague's presence in the Chiswick area at the time of his death, namely that he was visiting his mother. If his only intention was to commit suicide, why did he choose to travel to Chiswick, when there were other stretches of the Thames much closer to home? And why did he do so on a return ticket if he had no plans to return? The answer, it is suggested, was to meet a friend or friends. Was he, perhaps, intending to visit one of the favourite haunts of the Duke of Clarence's barrister friends? This was the home of Harry Wilson, of whom H. L. Stephen was later to write in an obituary: "During this period (1885-88) he was able to carry out an idea that he had long had in his mind by establishing a 'chummery' in a picturesque little house called The Osiers . . . where a succession of young men, chiefly from Cambridge, found an ideal substitute for the lonely and uncomfortable lodgings which would otherwise have been their lot, and where other friends could always find youthful and cheerful company."

Did Montague John Druitt visit the Osiers on the day of his death in December 1888? And if so, did he go voluntarily to this death or was he overpowered and murdered to prevent a public trial that would have destroyed some of the highest in the land? The questions have to be asked, for the home of fellow barrister Harry Wilson, one of Prince Eddy's closest friends, stood beside the River Thames at Chiswick Mall, adjacent to Thorneycroft Wharf, where Druitt's weighted corpse was pulled from the water.

The location of Druitt's death could, of course, be just another in the extraordinary series of coincidences that appear to link most of the leading Ripper candidates. Are they really coincidences or is there some substance in the claims of a cover-up at the highest level? Despite the claims of Howells and Skinner, the case against M. J. Druitt has not been proved. It is based on a mixture of hearsay, speculation, and circumstantial evidence. But equally it cannot be dismissed as some have tried to dismiss it. The police had some reason for thinking that Jack the Ripper had committed suicide soon after the last murder. Macnaghten had some reason for including Druitt's name in his notes and for suggesting that his family believed him to be the killer.

Perhaps one day we shall know the truth about Montague John Druitt's life and death. Perhaps then we will also know the true identity of Jack the Ripper. Or perhaps it is destined to remain one of the most intriguing murder mysteries of all time.

Montague John Druitt . . . was he Jack the Ripper?

8

The Car at Cloud's Hill

The mystery of a famous fatality, 1935

On a May morning in 1935 one of the world's most powerful motorcycles made its last journey along the country road leading northwards from Bovington Camp. The roar of the Brough Superior was heard by two young cyclists as it approached them from behind. Without looking back, they moved into single file and pedalled on. Seconds later, the motorcycle was seen "twisting and turning over and over" before coming to rest on the road. The two boys had been knocked off their cycles by the impact and found themselves on the ground. One was dazed and lapsed into unconsciousness but later recovered; his companion was unhurt. The condition of the motorcyclist was much more serious. He had not been wearing a crash helmet and his injuries included a nine-inch fracture of the skull and severe brain damage. He survived, unconscious, for six days in the military hospital at Bovington Camp. On the seventh day he died.

Two days later, a seven-man inquest jury, which included soldiers stationed at Bovington, filed into the military hospital to consider the circumstances surrounding the death of Lawrence of Arabia. Despite one "rather unsatisfactory" conflict of evidence concerning the possible involvement of an unidentified black car, the coroner observed that the circumstances were not such as to cause the jury any difficulty. They did not and the verdict was speedily delivered, the jurers concluding that Lawrence's death was an accident. But was it? Or was there something more sinister behind the sudden and dramatic demise of a military genius and national hero at a time when the war drums of Europe were being beaten against a backcloth of rising fascism and German rearmament?

Thomas Edward Lawrence was born at Tremadoc, Caernarvonshire, in 1888, the second of five sons of an Anglo-Irish artistocrat and the family governess. When he was eight, the family settled in Oxford and it was also in this city that he pursued a brilliant academic career, which included a major study of crusader castles in Syria and which led to a first-class honours degree in 1910. He returned to Syria the following year to take part in an archaeological dig at the lost city of Carchemish and by 1913 had become an expert photographer and surveyor with a working knowledge of Arabic. The qualifications were ideal for his next roles, conducting a survey of the Sinai Desert for Field Marshal Kitchener without arousing the suspicion of the ruling Turks, who thought he and his colleague were still engaged in archaeology, and, at the outbreak of war in 1914, work as an intelligence officer in Cairo.

But it was his achievements as leader of the Arab revolt that turned Lawrence into a living legend by the end of World War I. Through his understanding of the Arabs, his ability to speak their language, and his willingness to adopt their dress and way of life, he was able to win the confidence of the Arabs and unite their many factions. The result was a cohesive Arab army capable of taking on the might of the Turks, who had declared war on the Allies in November 1914. By a combination of guerilla tactics and brilliant strategy, Lawrence led his tribesmen to a number of victories that greatly assisted the Allied cause. He returned to Britain at the end of the war to a hero's welcome, which he was reluctant to accept. For the rest of his life he maintained a complex relationship with publicity, appearing at times to court it, yet also shunning it, actively seeking lowly rank and twice changing his name to escape public attention and the relentless newshounds of Fleet Street. As Sir Winston Churchill, a friend of Lawrence from their first meeting in 1919, put it, he had an extraordinary knack of "backing into the limelight".

After four months as Aircraftman John Hume Ross of the Royal Air Force, the former Colonel Lawrence enlisted as Trooper Thomas Edward Shaw in the Tank Corps, which was based at Bovington Camp. A few months later, in September 1923, he moved into a former gamekeeper's cottage at Cloud's Hill, a mile north of the army camp. It was to be his home until 1926 and again from 1929, when he bought the freehold for £450, until his death. It provided a perfect rural retreat from an army he described as "muck, stink and an abomination". It also served as a base for his other activities, which included correspondence with many of the great literary, artistic, and political figures of the day and visits to Thomas and Florence Hardy's home at Max Gate, Dorchester.

Lawrence's time in the Tank Corps was not a happy one, however, and in 1925 he was threatening to commit suicide unless he was

Lawrence the Arabian. *(Picture: National Portrait Gallery)*

Lawrence at Miranshah, on the Afghan border.

allowed to transfer back to the RAF. The ploy was successful and by the end of 1926 he was on his way to a posting in India's troubled Northwest Frontier District, close to the Afghan border, where soon rumours were afoot that he was involved in a spying mission. According to some Press reports, he was the "arch-spy of the world", training guerillas and making secret forays into Afghanistan. The stories were no more than speculation, but they served to bring about a rapid end to Lawrence's service in India. By February 1929, he was back in Britain.

The same year, still in the RAF, in which he remained until February 1935, Lawrence began working in Southampton Water, where he became involved in the development of power launches needed by the service for target-towing and air-sea rescue work. He also helped to manage the 1929 Schneider Cup seaplane races over the Solent, during which he succeeded in offending Lord Thomson, the Air Minister in the new Labour Government. He was also seen in conversation with such eminent people as the Marshal of the Italian Air Force and Nancy Astor, then a Tory MP for Plymouth. Lord Thomson subsequently decreed that it was inappropriate for a humble aircraftman to associate with "great men" and ordered that, if he wished to remain in the RAF, he must desist. In the event, the restriction was short-lived, as Thomson was one of the forty-four people killed in the R101 airship disaster in 1930.

Nevertheless, the limelight continued to follow Lawrence's every step and he was rarely out of it for long. He found himself accused at one of Stalin's show trials in Moscow of having plotted the overthrow of the Soviet Government. And, early in 1931, he was one of the first on the scene after an Irish flying-boat crashed, killing six of the twelve men on board. Some at least of the victims might have survived if a faster boat had been available and Lawrence used the tragedy to wage a personal campaign for better equipment, even publicly threatening to leave the RAF if he could not pursue his ideas. The Press took up the cause, an embarrassed Air Ministry acquiesced, and Aircraftman Shaw was able to spend his last two years of RAF service attached to civilian boatyards working on a new generation of high-speed launches, whose descendants were to save many lives in World War II.

In the closing weeks of 1934, Thomas Edward Shaw, alias Lawrence of Arabia, was preparing for his retirement from the RAF. It was due to begin in March 1935, when, as he wrote to one friend, he would become a "private citizen" and "shall have the honour and difficulty of paying for myself". During his Christmas leave, 1934, he discussed with his friend and neighbour at Cloud's Hill his plans to set up a private printing press there, in a shed which would need to be erected for the purpose. The proposed inaugural project was a limited edition of his then unpublished manuscript "The Mint", a damning account of life at the RAF depot in Uxbridge, where he had spent two months undergoing basic training in 1922, and of the brutal and degrading treatment meted out to recruits. Publication would not have been welcomed by the RAF. They had known of the manuscript for some years and had a secret file of "precautions for preventing publication of The Mint".

Lawrence began his retirement in a style to which he was unaccustomed. On February 26, 1935, the traveller more commonly associated with camels and fast motorcycles headed south from RAF Bridlington, North Humberside, on a bicycle. Without his service pay, he declared, he would have to "give up the luxury of running a high-powered motor cycle".

The Press were already convinced that there was more to Lawrence's future than quiet rural retirement. On February 13, two weeks before his departure from Bridlington, he wrote to a friend that the "Air

Ministry warns me that the Press are getting curious about my movements again. Damn the Press."

On March 6, during a break from his long cycle ride from Bridlington to Cloud's Hill, he wrote to Thomas Hardy's widow, Florence: "I should like to call but cannot. The Press-people are snooping round Cloud's Hill, taking its picture and looking for me, to take mine. So I will have to keep up in London and the Midlands for the next few weeks. As soon as I safely can I want to settle down in the little cottage for a long spell, and try to find out what there is left for me now the RAF is ended."

The Dorset cottage was still under seige when Lawrence finally returned there later in the month. He was so angered by one reporter that he planted a fist in his eye. And he was so desperate to be left alone that he went straight back to London to make personal appeals to the nation's Press barons and leading freelance agencies. But on his return from this trip, he found the situation unchanged and penned a letter to Esmond Harmsworth, chairman of the Newspaper Proprietors' Association.

"Unfortunately," he wrote, "the quietude has been a complete failure. Reporters and Press photographers have visited the place in some numbers, anxious to photograph it and me, or to ascertain my future intentions. This is a very simple district and their enquiries after me have given my country neighbours only too much to talk about. Their eagerness to find me drove me out; and after I had gone it led them to break the tiles of my roof, split the door and trample all over my patch of land in search of me. I have had to ask the local police to patrol the place, in my absence. I am writing to ask if your association can help to relieve me of some of this attention? I quite realise that many of the visitors are freelances: but even these find their market in the biggest newspapers. It would be a great comfort to me if editors could generally deny me further space."

Lawrence does appear to have been granted a limited respite from Press attention in the last weeks of his life, but there were times when his movements were being observed and even he was not aware of it. The most startling evidence of this emerged in 1968 in a letter published in the second issue of the *Dorset County Magazine*. In it, the writer of the letter, John Prentice, of Fareham, Hampshire, recalled what he described as a "real mystery", which occurred at Bovington on May 11, 1935.

"My friend Duncan Montagu Cake and I were serving with the RAOC and undergoing a tank recovery course at Cloud's Hill, near Wool, in Dorset," he wrote. "My Sealyham bitch, Gin, was in camp with me, and she was connected with the incident. It was a beautiful sunny afternoon, a Saturday, when we were off duty, and being country lovers it was decided to 'across the bracken and swamps' to Moreton, just to see the house where Lawrence of Arabia had his home.

"Suitably dressed, we had gone a mile or so, when Gin sniffed out an object partially covered by bracken. Closer inspection revealed a dustbin, the large type used by occupants of military married quarters. It could only have been manually carried over the swamp as the road, lined with rhododendrons leading to Moreton, was a long way away. In the far distance, Monty and I saw only a lady with a dog – nothing or nobody else.

"I removed the dustbin lid and took out a parcel, neatly tied with string, which I untied, throwing the string some distance away in the undergrowth. By this time, my friend was doing something similar with a second parcel in the bin. Mine contained a neatly folded civilian suit, shirt and socks. His had other items of male underwear and a trilby hat, also pressed. There was no footwear. Inside the hat was clearly inked the name 'Peter Page'.

"Bearing in mind that in those days there were some 'queer people' about, we allowed Gin to have a sniff, then replaced the wrapping minus the string, carrying on to our rendezvous – Moreton House. We made our way back by a different route, arriving at Cloud's Hill as our officers were at dinner in their Marquee Mess. We contacted Mr Beahan, who was orderly officer.

"The day was still bright and warm and Mr Beahan suggested we go back to the dustbin – if it were still there – then he would report our discovery to the local policeman. We went back, and imagine our surprise when there was no dustbin, and also no string! Somewhere, hidden, the mysterious dustbin owner had been watching us.

"We told Lieutenant Beahan, and as far as he was concerned the incident was closed. But not as far as Monty Cake and I were concerned! On the Sunday morning we reported to the local Military Police, and after their extensive inquiries we were told by them that 'No Peter Page was known locally'.

"Although nearly33 years have passed, the memory and the details are vivid, and I often wonder 'Who was Peter Page?' and what the . . . . . . was he up to!"

One might equally well ask what Lawrence himself was doing to attract such interest. With war clouds gathering on the horizon, a man of his fame, background, and particular brand of genius would inevitably be in demand from the political and the military figures of the day. One person who wished to see him was his friend Nancy Astor, Britain's first woman MP, who invited him to visit her home at Clivedon on May 25 to discuss the upheaval that would result from the proposal to "reorganize the defence forces". Lady Astor moved in the highest political circles and recogized Lawrence's potential in the current climate, but he politely excused himself. In a letter dated May 8, he told her: "No, wild mares would not at present take me away from Cloud's Hill. Also there is something broken in the works, as I told you: my will, I think. In this mood I would not take on any job at all, so do not commit yourself to advocating me, lest I prove a non-starter."

Another person anxious to see Lawrence in the light of recent political developments was Henry Williamson, author of *Tarka the Otter*, which had won him the Hawthornden Prize in 1928. Williamson was a committed follower of Mosley's British Union of Fascists and in early May 1935 he wrote to Lawrence asking if he could come to Dorset. His plan, as he apparently made clear in the letter, was to invite the hero of Arabia to go to Germany to meet Adolf Hitler and "send him along the proper track". He recognized that public support from Lawrence would add greatly to the credibility of the British Fascists; he hoped that Lawrence's intervention might even help to prevent a war between Britain and Germany.

It was not the first time that Lawrence had been approached by the Fascist movement. Hitler's supporters made direct contact with him on more than one occasion in the early 1930s and in 1934 Lawrence told Liddell Hart that the "Fascists had been after him" but that he had rejected their offers. Henry Williamson received neither an acceptance nor a rejection of his proposals, but he interpreted Lawrence's initial response as something more than encouraging.

On the morning of Monday May 13, 1935, Lawrence asked his neighbour, Mrs Knowles, if she would be good enough to prepare a meal for a visitor, whom he was planning to invite to Cloud's Hill the following day. She agreed and soon afterwards he set off on his motorcycle, heading for Bovington Camp. There he went to the Post Office and despatched a brief telegram: "11.25 AM 13 MAY 1935. WILLIAMSON SHALLOWFORD FILLEIGH. LUNCH TUESDAY WET FINE. COTTAGE 1 MILE NORTH OF BOVINGTON CAMP." (The reference to the weather was obviously prompted by the intimation in Williamson's initiatory letter that he would only come if it was fine.)

While he was at the camp, Lawrence also bought two chops from the Bovington Butcher, F. J. Stratton, and told him he had to be going because he would be spending the afternoon on the road to Catterick Camp in North Yorkshire, where he had to report by 5 p.m. At first sight, it appears to be a puzzling remark from someone who, only twenty-four hours earlier, had written to a friend in Oxford that he was "sitting in my cottage and getting used to an empty life", and who was intending, twenty-four hours later, to entertain a guest for lunch. Was Lawrence really intending to ride his motorcycle to Yorkshire and back in twenty-four hours? The answer is unknown.

However, we have to remember that Lawrence had undertaken many far more arduous journeys during his 46 years, had recently travelled from Yorkshire to Dorset on a bicycle, albeit with a number of lengthy stops on the way, and that his greatest joy was riding his Brough Superior. It was the world's fastest motorcycle and Lawrence, an expert rider, rode it at speed and often over long distances. He once described how, having been freed from his army fatigues at Bovington by 10 a.m. one Easter weekend, he "leaped for my bike and raced her madly up the London road: Wimborne, Ringwood, Romsey, Winchester, Basingstoke, Bagshot, Staines, Hounslow by 1.20 p.m. (three hours less five minutes). Good for 125 miles: return journey took 10 minutes less!"

In another letter written in 1923, Lawrence admitted: "When my mood gets too hot and I find myself wandering beyond control, I pull out my motorbike and hurl it at top speed through these unfit roads for hour after hour. My nerves are jaded and gone dead, so that nothing less than hours of voluntary danger will prick them into life: and the 'life' they reach then is melancholy joy at risking something worth exactly 2 shillings 9 pence a day."

Whether it really was Lawrence's intention to ride to Catterick and back before entertaining his guest, we can only guess. He was the kind of man who, far from being deterred by the rigours of such an ambitious two-way journey, would have relished the prospect of it, especially if he had a pressing reason for undertaking it. Whether there was such a reason, and whether it was connected with the proposed visit of Williamson the following day, again we can only guess.

In the event, Lawrence failed to arrive at Catterick or even at his Cloud's Hill cottage. The accident occurred 400 yards from his home and Lawrence and the injured cyclist were taken in an army lorry to Bovington Camp hospital where they were admitted "between 11.30 and 11.45 a.m."

From this point on, the full facts of the whole tragic affair became clouded by a cloak of official secrecy. The Air Ministry was involved from the outset and in hospital the unconscious Lawrence was guarded by two Special Branch detectives, one constantly at his bedside. On the day after the accident, the *Daily Express* quoted a hospital spokesman as saying: "All I am permitted to tell is that we have in the hospital a Mr Shaw. We have strict instructions to give no other information. No, I cannot say how he is."

The key witness to the accident, Corporal Ernest Catchpole, of the Royal Army Ordnance Corps, who saw the motorcycle swerve and heard the crash, was warned by his superior officers at Bovington Camp not to give information to the Press. At the same time, and before the police inquiries into the crash had even begun, a statement was issued from the camp that there were no witnesses. All military personnel at Bovington were warned that the passing of any information to the Press would constitute a breach of the Official Secrets Act and warnings were also given to at least one and probably both the cyclists, who were both the sons of serving soldiers. On May 16, the *Dorset Daily Echo* published an interview with Frank Fletcher, the uninjured boy, about the accident – but this appears to have been set up by the authorities in order to quell the mounting speculation about its cause. On May 17, the same newspaper informed its readers that on the day after the accident, military and civil police had "called on the father and told him that on no account was the boy to be interviewed without authority".

It was an extraordinary level of secrecy for a man who was supposed to have severed his ties with the RAF two months previously and was now a civilian living quietly in retirement and "getting used to an empty life". Inevitably, the secrecy fuelled speculation and aroused the suspicions of the Press. The *Daily Sketch* reported that the credentials of all who approached the hospital were being carefully scrutinized and the *Daily Mirror* claimed that the father of Albert Hargreaves, the injured cyclist, was refused permission to see him for two days even though his condition was comfortable.

"Why are such extraordinary precautions being taken in the case of Lawrence?" asked the *Mirror*. General Allenby, who knew the injured man well, told them he had no idea. The following day, the same newspaper reported that Lawrence's Cloud's Hill cottage was being heavily guarded in order to "safeguard vital Air Ministry documents which Mr Shaw had in his possession".

A further mystery had also now been placed in the arena, namely that of a mysterious black car said to have been seen travelling towards Lawrence's motorcycle as he approached the two cyclists. The *Daily Mail* reported: "Apparently, he swerved to avoid the car, and he wrenched his machine into the banking to minimise the impact with the cyclists."

Lawrence's brother, Arnold, who flew back from a holiday in Majorca within twenty-four hours of the accident, did his best to dispel the rumour and speculation.

"All this mystery about my brother's recent movements and work has little basis in fact," he told the *Mail*. "So far as I know he had no connection with any Government department, nor was he doing any Government work. Whatever Secret Service work he may have done is finished now."

Sadly, the last sentence was only too true. The injuries that Lawrence of Arabia had sustained were such that, if he had lived, some of the functions of his brain would have been seriously impaired. He would have been paralysed, unable to speak, blind in his left eye, and would also have suffered loss of memory. In the event, after lingering unconscious for six days, and despite the attention of the nation's top specialists, he died soon after 8 a.m. on the morning of May 19. The cause of death was given as congestion of the lungs and heart following a fracture of the skull and laceration of the brain.

The necessary formalities following Lawrence's death were arranged and carried out with a haste that bordered on the indecent. The inquest was held on the morning of May 21, the funeral later the same day. At the inquest, held in a dining room at the military hospital, Corporal Catchpole recalled that he was on the camping ground about a hundred yards from the road at Cloud's Hill when he heard Lawrence's motorcycle coming from Bovington Camp at a speed which he estimated at 50 to 60 m.p.h.

Asked by the coroner if he saw any other vehicle, he said: "The motorcycle passed a black car when it was about level with the camp. The car, which was a private one, was going in the opposite direction and the motorcycle got passed it all right. Then I saw the motorcycle swerve across the road to avoid two pedal cyclists coming from Bovington. It swerved immediately after it had passed the car. The next thing I heard was a crash. I saw the bike twisting and turning over and over along the road. I saw nothing of the driver."

Catchpole said that he ran to the scene and found the motorcyclist on the road, his face covered with blood. He tried to wipe away the blood with handkerchiefs and sent to the camp for a stretcher. Then an Army Service Corps lorry came along and he asked the driver to take the motorcyclist to hospital. One of the pedal cyclists was lying some distance down the road.

Asked by the coroner if there was sufficient room for the motorcyclist to pass between the car and the cyclists, Catchpole replied: "There would have been if the motor cyclist had not been going at such a speed."

Both Frank Fletcher and Albert Hargreaves emphatically denied any knowledge of the black car referred to by Catchpole. Hargreaves rememberd nothing at all after hearing the sound of the approaching motorcycle, but Fletcher recalled the accident in detail. He said Hargreaves was cycling behind him when he heard Lawrence's machine.

"I heard a crash and Bert's bicycle fell on top of me," he said. "I was knocked off. I got up and saw Mr Lawrence go over his handlebars."

Catchpole's certainty about the black car and the boys' equal certainty that they did not see it continued to puzzle the coroner and the jury alike.

"It seems a funny thing how the car was not seen," said one juror, adding that the cyclists may have left the road and ridden for a way across the common. The boys denied this. Before the jury delivered its verdict, the coroner made a further reference to the "conflicting point in the evidence" relating to the car, which he described as "rather unsatisfactory".

The mystery of the black car has haunted the Lawrence legend for half-a-century but now perhaps this ghost at least may be laid to rest. In response to an article commemorating the 50th anniversary of Lawrence's death in 1985, an elderly Wimborne woman, Mrs Margaret Montague, wrote a brief letter to the *Bournemouth Evening Echo*. It contained a startling revelation about the car.

"I can assure you there definitely was a car," she wrote, "and it was a black one. The registration number was COW 41 and I know who was driving it. The driver and Lawrence waved to each other as they passed."

Later, Mrs Montague told reporter David Radcliff that the driver was in fact her late husband, Lionel.

"I know it has been a mystery - that is why I thought I would lay this one for good and all if I can," she said. "I don't know whether he was on his way to or coming back from Bovington Camp, and he waved to Mr Shaw. He had told me before that that bike would be the death of Mr Shaw. It was an awful-looking thing, sinister-looking. My husband and he were quite friendly - they used to talk each other. When my husband got to the garage at Sandford, he spoke to Mr Hope and they had just heard about the accident. My husband said: 'I don't think so - because I've just waved to him.' It must have happened seconds after my husband waved to him. My husband always said that Mr Shaw swerved to avoid that butcher's boy. It was a treacherous bit of road in those days."

Can we now conclude, therefore, that the mystery of the black car, which has taunted two generations of investigators, has at last been solved? Perhaps, but at least two questions about the car remain unanswered. One concerns the claim by another student of the case, journalist Colin Graham, that a week before the accident, Lawrence and an airman friend, both on motorcycles, noticed a black car apparently being tested on the road which ran past his cottage, the implication being that it was a test run for what later happened. The other concerns the failure of Lionel Montague to make himself known at the time, despite the widespread publicity given to the accident and to the unidentified vehicle. Mr Montague is no longer alive to tell us why he did not come forward and his widow, having made her revelation, has since declared that she has said all she intends to say on the matter.

Other mysteries also remain. So too do theories about the cause of the fatal accident at Cloud's Hill. Was Lawrence's death a "quasi-suicide", in which he consciously decided to sacrifice his own life to save the boys? The suggestion has been made by at least one author, based on letters written by Lawrence that suggest that he was depressed and directionless following his "retirement" from the RAF. On the other hand, the letters are equally consistent with the alternative claim that he was deliberately trying to give his friends and acquaintances the impression of aimlessness in order to distract them from some secret work in which he may have been involved.

The quasi-suicide theory seems somewhat far-fetched. The claim that Lawrence "sacrificed his own life" to save the boys says no more than that he took evasive action in an attempt to avoid them, which is surely what any motorist or motorcyclist would do in an emergency of this kind. In fact, Lawrence did not even succeed in avoiding them, both boys being knocked off their bicycles and one being knocked unconscious.

A more imaginative theory, though an equally unlikely one, is that Lawrence's death was faked in order that he might retire in peace, perhaps to Morocco. The only evidence to support this is that photographs were taken of Lawrence in his coffin but none of them came out.

By far the most popular of the non-accident theories is that Lawrence of Arabia was murdered. A colourful array of candidates have been nominated as suspects, among them the Germans (concerned that Lawrence might be taking over the reorganisation of Britain's home defences), the French (seeking to avenge his anti-French activities), the Russian Bolsheviks (fearing Lawrence's alleged

Lawrence the English colonel.

activities as the "arch-spy of the world"), the IRA (Lawrence turned down the chance to lead a brigade in the Free State army), the Arabs (over British betrayals following the Arab revolt), and the British secret service (worried that he might become a Blackshirt or publish his RAF memoirs).

Supporters of the foul-play theory have included Colin Graham, who has devoted much research time to the subject, and Henry Williamson, who was due to meet Lawrence on the day following the crash at Cloud's Hill. Williamson was convinced (perhaps optimistically) that Lawrence's positive response to his request to meet him amounted to an acceptance of his plan for a meeting with Adolf Hitler. He also noted that his last letter to Lawrence—the one that led to the telegram—was never found and must therefore have been secretly removed from the Cloud's Hill cottage at some time after the accident.

The foul-play theory appears to have more going for it than do its quasi-suicide and faked-death rivals. What exactly caused Lawrence to collide with the cyclists has never become clear. Corporal Catchpole's evidence suggests that Lawrence was travelling fairly fast (as he often did), which would have made it more difficult to control the machine in an emergency. Yet Lawrence was an experienced and expert motorcyclist, whose skill on two wheels was admired by many, including George Brough, the manufacturer of his Brough Superior. It has been suggested that the cyclists were hidden in a dip in the road, but the police evidence about the precise location of the accident appears to rule this out. Rodney Legg estimates that Lawrence would have been able to see the boys as much as half-a-mile away. Perhaps the crash was caused by mechanical failure: the motorcycle was found afterwards to be jammed in second gear. Perhaps Lawrence's riding was affected in some way by the black car as it passed. Mrs Montague claimed that her husband exchanged waves with Lawrence and it is possible that this affected his concentration. Or perhaps the car's driver made some kind of driving error, which might also explain why he never came forward.

Such matters are for a coroner and jury to consider, but at the inquest into Lawrence's death, some aspects were barely touched upon and others totally ignored. After initially claiming that there were no independent witnesses, the authorities did at least put Corporal Catchpole on the stand. But there was no hint of other witnesses, which is surprising when one looks at the discoveries made by Lawrence biographer Michael Yardley as recently as 1980-81, when he was stationed at Bovington. Yardley spent many afternoons with Pat Knowles and his wife and was introduced to an elderly man, whom he calls "L. C.", who did not wish to become embroiled in the Lawrence mystery and "had never publicised his presence near the scene of the crash, although it was no secret to the camp authorities".

Yardley writes: "On 13 May, L. C. , then a teenager, was working

Lawrence's Brough Superior at the Wareham Museum.

as 'mate' to a Mr O'Conner, local lorry driver, who had been contracted by the Army to help 'clear the gear' from an Army training camp. While L. C. and Mr O'Conner were loading the lorry, they heard the crash and ran to the spot, arriving just after Catchpole. They saw an overturned motorbike on the side of the road. This was the eastern side of the road, and therefore Lawrence was, as the boys and Catchpole later testified, on the wrong side of the road. A little way in front of the bike a man was lying in a pool of blood. L. C. recognised him and said, 'It's Lawrence.' O'Conner, noticing the blood pouring from the side of the victim's head, remarked, 'He's done for.' At this point Lawrence, who had appeared unconscious, opened his eyes and, looking directly upward towards L. C., O'Conner and Catchpole, brought up his hand and held out a finger as if to indicate the number one – then he lapsed back into unconsciousness.''

Was Lawrence's last act the dying gesture of a Moslem, his raised finger indicating that there is only one God? Was he trying to convey some more sinister message, perhaps about the black car? Both solutions are suggested by Yardley, who adds to the confusion with a footnote casting doubt upon the reliability of his source. However, the footnote also reaffirms his claim that two important witnesses were not called to the inquest.

The strongest argument against the murder theory is that it would have been extremely difficult to plan a road accident of the kind that happened (how could you ensure that all the participants were in the right place at the right time?) and impossible to ensure that they all played their parts in the way intended (Lawrence might have avoided both the black car and the cyclists). And even if there were a collision, there could be no guarantee either that the intended victim would be killed or that other participants would survive. A would-be killer could, of course, tamper with the victim's vehicle but there is no evidence that this happened in Lawrence's case, the only known mechanical defect being the jammed gearbox.

The various theories that there was something sinister about Lawrence's death owe as much to the veil of official secrecy surrounding it as they do to hard evidence. Both the Press and the public enjoy a good mystery, Lawrence – in death as in life – was the perfect person to provide it and the authorities seem to have been intent on adding to it. But why? Why were the authorities so determined to prevent people speaking publicly about the accident? Why did they find it necessary to guard both the unconscious Lawrence and his cottage and possessions so thoroughly? Why did they convene the inquest so hastily that two important witnesses were overlooked? Or was there a more sinister reason for their absence from the witness box?

The Air Ministry's warning to Lawrence that the Press were "getting curious" about his movements in February 1935 suggest that the inordinate level of official interest predates the Cloud's Hill accident by several months at least. The discovery of clothes in a dustbin and their rapid removal also raises questions about the official interest. Peter Page— the name found in the clothing—was also the name of one of Britain's most successful investigative journalists. Was he also, as Rodney Legg suggests, an MI5 agent using journalism as a cover?

One clue to the reason for the official interest in Lawrence even after his retirement may lie in his neighbour Pat Knowles' statement that their plans to print a limited edition of *The Mint* at Cloud's Hill early in 1935 fell through because Lawrence was about to become involved in "government work". A second clue may lie in the published diaries of Colonel Richard Meinertzhagen, an old friend in whom Lawrence had confided in the past. In his *Middle East Diary*, Meinertzhagen reveals that, in May 1935, Lawrence headed a review panel considering the entire restructuring of the British intelligence services.

"We worked together in the Cabinet Office on a Scheme for a Directorship of Intelligence embracing both political and military aspects and coalescing under one head Foreign Office, War Office, Admiralty, Air Ministry, Scotland Yard and MI5," writes Meinertzhagen. "Put the thing to Churchill, Amery, Macdonogh, they concurred. Involved training college in London and one in the country. It was complete and we were applying for Treasury sanction when TE died. I felt I could not go on with it as it was very much his work."

Was the man fatally injured at Cloud's Hill, Dorset, on May 13, 1935, really England's master spy, as the contemporary German newspapers claimed? If Meinertzhagen's statement is true—and we have no reason to doubt that it is—it appears that the Germans were not exaggerating. Lawrence had the experience in such matters, he had the qualifications, and he had the contacts, as was evident at his funeral at nearby Moreton on May 21. Heading the procession was another of Lawrence's influential friends, Winston Churchill. Two days earlier, the man who was later to lead Britain through World War II had commented: "We have lost one of the greatest beings of our time. I hoped to see him quit his retirement and take a commanding part in facing the dangers which now threaten our country."

Do the words of Churchill amount to a further hint that there was more to Lawrence's final months than most were able or willing to admit? Herein lies one of the greatest and most authentic of the many mysteries that have surrounded the life and death of Lawrence of Arabia; and because of its nature, it is one which may one day be solved.

And so to the mystery of the flowers, the famous bunch of white roses delivered annually to Moreton Rectory. They arrive on August 16, acknowledged by Lawrence as his true birthday, though his birth certificate stated August 15. A Weymouth florist makes the delivery, but the order comes from America, placed by an unknown customer. Each year the rector places the roses on Lawrence's grave and each year there is one rose less. If this diminishing rate is maintained, the last rose will arrive in the year 2020. Will the sender by then be known? The most popular candidate hitherto is Nancy Astor, the most likely Lawrence's Californian admirer Theodora Duncan. But perhaps this most harmless of the Lawrence mysteries is also the one that needs least to be solved.

9

The Winton Wrecker
The mystery of the Abbott Road poltergeist, 1981

In most respects, Friday August 14, 1981, began normally for the Burden family of Abbott Road, Winton, Bournemouth. The head of the household, Charles Burden, set off as usual for his work as a window cleaner, unaware that his family's normally peaceful existence was about to be shattered in a way that he would not have thought possible. There was one early sign that everything was not as it should be when, at 5 a.m. the family's thirteen-year-old black labrador, Panda, began howling. But Mr Burden ignored it, assuming that the animal had been disturbed by cats. It did not occur to him that Panda was reacting to some strange supernatural power—a power that would shortly throw his family into turmoil and plunge them under the media spotlight on an international scale.

Living with Mr Burden at 37 Abbott Road were his wife, Kathy, who suffered from Huntington's chorea (at the time it was thought her complaint was multiple sclerosis), their seventeen-year-old adopted daughter, Deborah, who worked as an auxiliary nurse, and their retarded foster son, Bradley, who was eight. Only Mrs Burden and Bradley were in the seventy-year-old detached house at 9 a.m. when vases and ornaments started flying across rooms and crockery began to jump off shelves.

"I was upstairs making the beds when I heard something downstairs," Mrs Burden told reporter Chris Adamson of the *Bournemouth Evening Echo* later that day. "It was two bottles of squash falling off a shelf in the kitchen. Then the table in the hall, with flowers on it, fell over. Everything was falling around. The television went up and fell over and all the things on the top fell off."

The destruction continued for an hour. Neighbours rushed round in response to Mrs Burden's cries for help. Her husband was sent for and arrived home at 9.30. He was immediately aware of a strange

122

Kathy Burden surveys the poltergeist's work in her kitchen. *(Photo: Duncan Lee, Evening Echo, Bournemouth)*

atmosphere. He described the house as "very cold" and himself as "very frightened". He decided to call the police. But as he lifted the receiver, it was inexplicably wrenched from his hand. Then a large paraffin heater suddenly flew from one side of the hall to the other and crashed into the wall. The table on which the telephone stood began to shake, throwing off a flower pot and other objects. In the lounge, the colour television set toppled on to its screen and a heavy gas fire fell forward from the grate.

Mr Burden eventually succeeded in contacting the police and the first two policemen to arrive were able to confirm the events. Sergeant Alan Woods estimated the temperature drop at 10° to 15° or more. Constable Graham Joyce said he heard Mrs Burden cry out that it was getting cold again. Then there was a terrific crash in the kitchen.

"There was a hell of a bang; then, as I came in, the kitchen cabinet was falling to the ground," said PC Joyce. "It was really eerie. There is no logical explanation for it. I've never believed these sort of things before but this is weird."

The kitchen cabinet had tipped its entire contents on to the floor. On police advice, a priest was sent for. Dr Frederick Oliver, assistant at St. Alban's Church, Bournemouth, arrived at noon to conduct a service of exorcism. The *Echo* reported: "Dr Oliver, a graduate from Yale and London universities, asked everyone to be quiet and as the house became peaceful for the first time yesterday, he prayed for the spirits to go away. After calling on the evil spirits to leave the house, he asked everyone to join in the Lord's Prayer. Satisfied that there would be no further trouble, Dr Oliver talked about the forces of evil that he felt coming from the room. 'There is something evil still in the house but I do not think it will manifest itself again,' he said."

According to the Burdens' only natural daughter, Mrs Noreen Penfold, of West Howe, Bournemouth, the priest also sprinkled "holy water" in the house, only to find that it came back in his face.

Later that day, several people took part in a seance at 37 Abbott Road. They included Mrs Penfold, who claims to be clairvoyant, Mrs Marie Nadin, who lived nearby in a house formerly occupied by the Burdens, and David Haith, a *Bournemouth Times* reporter who had a special interest in the paranormal. In his report the following week, Haith described how Mrs Nadin began "shaking and mumbling."

"Seated with two mediums and others round a greenhouse table," he wrote, "I suddenly saw Mrs Nadin take on a tortured expression and cry out, 'Go away'. Then one medium comforted her and asked the spirit—thought to be of a neighbour who hanged himself—to 'join with them in the brighter world'. After several minutes, Mrs Nadin

Charles and Kathy Burden with Dr. Frederick Oliver who performed an exorcism at 37 Abbott Road. *(Photo: Duncan Lee, Evening Echo, Bournemouth)*

shuddered and came out of the 'trance' and rested her head on the table, exhausted."

Afterwards, Mrs Nadin told Haith: "I was frightened. I felt that someone was making me do what I didn't want to do. There was something within me that wasn't me. But towards the end everything was getting lighter. Nothing like this has ever happened to me before. I've never thought of myself as a medium."

The night of August 14, 1981, was a peaceful one at 37 Abbott Road and it began to appear that Dr Oliver's belief that the "evil" would not manifest itself again might be justified. But at 9 o'clock the following morning, the destruction began again. It was a Saturday morning and Debbie Burden was still in bed. She said later: "My mother and Bradley were downstairs when a milk bottle crashed to the floor. Then when I was downstairs all the things on the television and a table fell off and the television fell over. It was only when Bradley and Mum went across the road that things stopped happening."

There was more drama later in the morning and again it was witnessed by outsiders, including a woman social worker who had called on the Burdens. She described how she was in the kitchen helping to make a pot of tea when things began to move around. Then, like the policemen a day earlier, she watched in amazement as a cabinet laden with food and crockery crashed to the ground.

"Things were crashing around and there was no explanation for it. Things were flying past us but not at us. They were whizzing round with terrific force," said the social worker.

For the second day running, a churchman was sent for. This time it was Mr Albert White of the Bath Road Spiritualist Church in Bournemouth, who decided to hold another seance. It was conducted in the lounge at 37 Abbott Road and involved eight people sitting round a table and attempting to communicate with the spirit world. David Haith was present again and the participants also included Debbie and Bradley.

Reporting that this time it was Debbie's turn to find herself "taken over", Haith went on: "One medium present clairvoyantly gave the surname of the neighbour who was hanged and mumbled, 'I didn't do it. I wouldn't do it,' and clutched his neck as if in pain. Then came the words, 'It's a child. It's all fun to them. Ian comes to play.' Bradley was then asked: 'Who is Ian?' And he replied: 'My friend.' It was then that Debbie began shaking and suddenly said: 'He's still here.' Then she giggled in a child's voice."

Kathy Burden was not present at this second seance but afterwards she and her husband revealed that Bradley did indeed have an imaginary playmate called Ian. The boy would talk to him in the garden, and offer him a kick of his football or a ride on his bike. But the couple were not worried by this. When they asked whom he was talking to, he would say: "Just somebody."

Describing her feelings during the seance, Debbie told reporters: "I suddenly felt cold. It kind of crept up from my feet. It was cold under the table and then my breathing got clearer and deeper. I felt something inside my stomach—I had this sharp feeling above my tummy—but when the medium questioned me I started giggling and went shy. I couldn't say anything because I felt shy. I didn't know what was going on but I felt like a child and wanted to laugh. Then Ian went through the medium and was able to speak to us."

Charles Burden said: "This spirit called to Bradley and laughed with him. He told us that he was nine years old and he was working through our daughter Deborah. We pictured him as being fair-haired. He spoke through the medium in a child's voice and said he was doing all these things for fun but he wouldn't tell us about himself. It was very strange. I have never believed in this sort of thing before but I will believe in it now."

The mediums advised the Burdens to leave the house for four days. Charles Burden moved to a boarding house, his wife went to stay with a friend at Portsmouth, Debbie stayed with neighbours, and Bradley stayed with Noreen Penfold at West Howe and later at a nearby children's home.

By this time the family and their experiences had become headline news in the newspapers and on television and radio. The *Daily Mirror* even arranged for a reporter and photographer to spend two days and nights in the deserted house. They set up their equipment in the hope that the ghost of Abbott Road would provide them with the scoop of the century.

"On both nights cameras were set up to cover entire rooms and take three pictures during every second of any possible poltergeist activity," wrote Alister Martin. "We set up tripwires so that any wandering spirits or pranksters would activate our cameras."

At one point the cameras were indeed activated, but the cause turned out to be not a wandering spirit but a wandering cat. The creature went on to bite the reporter as he brandished the crucifix given to him by Charles Burden for protection. In the excitement his cameraman colleague cut his hand on a piece of broken glass on the floor. Apart from that, Martin was forced to report, all was quiet at 37 Abbott Road. Neither of the Mirrormen heard or felt any evidence of the supernatural during their two-day stay.

Another visitor to the abandoned building was Miriam Jeffreys, from Southampton, who claimed to have been told by a white witch that she had special powers. She arrived, as the *Echo* put it, "carrying a Bible and wooden cross and clothed in a shining white dress, like an avenging angel". Her request to meet Bradley was turned down by Mr Burden but he allowed her inside the house and afterwards reported that she "talked a lot of sense". After placing pictures of Kathy Burden, Deborah, and Bradley between the pages of her leather-bound Bible, she said that there was now no reason why the family could not return to their home.

The Burdens and the authorities were inundated with both Press inquiries and offers of help from mediums and other psychic specialists. One approach to the Dorset police, made through a Hampshire colleague, came from a woman said to be "high up in Government circles", who expressed her willingness to help with the Abbott Road situation as long as there was no risk of publicity. A senior Dorset officer, who was involved in the Winton case, recalls: "I replied that the Press were already having a field day and 'no publicity'

Charles Burden with Miriam Jeffreys. *(Photo: Duncan Lee, Evening Echo, Bournemouth.)*

was the last thing I could guarantee. What interested me was that the woman also asked if there was a mentally retarded or handicapped child in the house. I replied that there was not and it was only later that I learned that the family had a foster son who was retarded."

As the story of the Burdens and their plight reached an audience of millions, speculation on the cause of the poltergeist activity became rife. Students of the paranormal noted that on the day before the opening events of the Abbott Road drama, many people in the same area of Winton had reported seeing a "huge, rumbling UFO" fly overhead. Did this constitute evidence to support the theory that ghosts and UFOs were in some way linked?

A local member of the Society for Psychical Research observed that the Abbott Road case was similar to that of the Enfield poltergeist, which plagued a family in their council house for fourteen months between 1977 and 1979. At the centre of the Enfield case, which involved a wide range of paranormal phenomena witnessed by a number of reliable witnesses and even a professional photographer's camera, was an eleven-year-old girl. It has long been recognized that a high proportion of such cases involve children on the verge of puberty, particularly girls.

There are a great many other precedents for the kind of events that happened in Abbott Road, Winton, in 1981. They have occurred throughout recorded history all over the world. Some incidents, including Enfield, have been extremely well-documented by highly credible witnesses such as professional investigators, writers, policemen, and other public officials. Each case is unique but striking similarities to other cases are often apparent. The sound of knocking, rapping, and footsteps, the movement of heavy furniture, objects flying through the air, and damage and destruction of various kinds are all typical symptoms of poltergeist activity. The activities often give the impression that they have been directed by an intelligence. Written messages have been known to appear and in some cases the intelligence even seems to have a sense of humour.

As a reporter with the *Bournemouth Evening Echo,* I covered several poltergeist incidents during the 1970s and early 1980s and found them both convincing and baffling. One involved a young couple in their twenties who had just taken over the Oddfellows Arms public house at Wimborne. On their first night in the ancient premises they worked late and did not retire to bed until 3 a.m. A couple of hours later, their guests in another room heard their screams as they awoke to find their bed moving from one side of the bedroom to the other. So violent was the movement that the young couple were thrown out of the bed and finished up underneath it, one of them with cuts and bruises to the arm. As far as I am aware there were no pubescent or retarded children in the house but there was one similarity to the Winton case—the connection with a suicide. A few year earlier, a former landlord of the Oddfellows Arms had hanged hmself at the nearby Dorset House pub, which he had just taken over.

Another publican who died an unnatural death was a former landlord of the Old Thatch at Uddens, near Ferndown. In the mid-1970s, I wrote a story about a temporary manager of the pub who had refused to spend a second night there after telling of furniture moving around in his room when there was no-one else in the building. It sounded like a possible poltergeist incident and while making inquiries about this, I learned that it was not the first mysterious event to occur at the Old Thatch. Some years before, the pub had had a Polish-born landlord who had died tragically after falling down the stairs. Two first-hand witnesses independently told how, ten days after his death, there was a minor explosion among the bottles in the bar, resulting in the glass letter "U" from the side of a Cointreau bottle flying across the bar area and landing at the feet of an employee with whom the late landlord had not enjoyed the best of relationships. A few days after that

129

incident, the same thing happened again, involving the same individual and the Cointreau bottle that had replaced the first one. A letter was sent to the manufacturers of Cointreau, who expressed their puzzlement and added that there was nothing in their product likely to cause such an explosion.

Dorset can also boast a famous Victorian poltergeist, which became active in 1894 at an isolated cottage at Norton, near the village of Durweston, three miles from Blandford. The cottage was occupied by a widow called Mrs Best, whom the *Western Gazette* described at the time as "a most respectable woman, of a quiet inoffensive disposition and on good terms with her neighbours and the village generally", and two orphan girls who had been boarded out to her by the Honourable Misses Pitt of Steepleton. The poltergeist announced its arrival on December 13, 1894, with faint knocking and scratching sounds in various parts of the cottage. Five days later, the next-door neighbour, Lord Portman's gamekeeper Mr Newman, was sent for after the elder girl, Anne Cleave, who was about thirteen, said she had seen a boot come from the garden and strike the back door. Sitting in Mrs Best's cottage, Newman watched in amazement as beads began to strike the window. He shouted back: "You're a coward. Why don't you throw money?" At this point the door opened itself, to fifteen inches from the wall, and a quantity of shells floated into the room.

Describing the incident later to an investigator from the Society for Psychical Research, Newman recalled: "They came one at a time, at intervals varying from half-a-minute; they came very slowly and when they hit me I could hardly feel them. With the shells came two thimbles, they came so slowly that in the ordinary way they would have dropped long before reaching me. The two children were all the time in the room with me. Then right from below me a slate pencil came as if from the copper and a hasp, like the hasp of my glove, was dropped on to my lap from a point above the level of my head. I never saw any of the things start to move. The time was somewhere between 10 and 11 a.m. on a nice clear day.

"A boot then came from outside the door. It came in moving a foot above the ground and pitched down. The boot had been lying right in front of the door, where it had previously fallen. It fell at my side. Mrs Best threw it out. After this I went out and put my foot on it and said, 'I defy anything to move this boot.' Just as I stepped off, it rose up behind me and knocked my hat off. There was no-one behind me. The boot and the hat fell down together."

A few days later, Mrs Best and the orphan girls went to stay in Newman's cottage, where, on January 10, they received a visit from the rector of Durweston, the Rev W. M. Anderson, and the village schoolmaster, Mr Sheppard. After the girls had gone to bed and while their foster mother was still upstairs with them, the two men heard loud rappings on the walls in different parts of the downstairs room in which they sat. The schoolmaster went outside to check that no one was playing tricks, while the rector remained indoors. He wrote later: "I put my ear and head to the wall, but could not detect any vibrations. But when resting my head on the rail at the bottom of the bed, I could distinctly feel a vibration varying according to the loudness of the knocking. Occasionally there was noise in the wall, as if someone were scratching with their nails. When the rapping first began, I noticed that it frequently ceased when I came into the room, but after a short time it made no difference and the noise was loud and continuous."

The poltergeist was offered a slate and some chalk, which were placed on the windowsill, and invited to communicate. It replied with a number of raps, which were taken to be a positive response, but would only make use of the slate when everyone except Mrs Best and the girls had left the bedroom and the light had been removed. It was 2.30 a.m.

Mr Anderson, who was listening under the stairs with other witnesses, recalled: "Amid perfect silence we all heard the pencil scratching the slate. The slightest movement by anyone in the bed would have been detected by me in a moment, and I am absolutely certain that the writing could not have been done by anyone in the room, without my knowing it. I told Mrs Best that I was myself convinced that no one had moved in the bed, much less left it, but people would say such had been the case. She said she was prepared to take a solemn oath that none of them had moved or left the bed, which was some four feet or more from the window."

The witnesses left the room five times and on each occasion there was more scratching on the slate. Once it produced some beautifully drawn curves and twice it responded with actual words—"MONY" (sic) and "GARDEN". But the phenomenon refused to be silent and its raps and noises continued to follow the sisters even when they were moved to a third house in the village.

Eventually the girls were separated. Anne was taken to Iwerne Minster, where the disturbances resumed once again. A large stone was thrown on to the porch roof and snowdrops were scattered around the garden. A board inspector arrived and took the girl to her flat in London for a week. Nothing significant occurred there and the inspector arranged for a doctor to examine the girl, with the result that she was pronounced to be hysterical and of a remarkably consumptive tendency. Her fate beyond this point is unknown.

The Durweston case, which was thoroughly investigated by the Society for Psychical Research, is a typical one in a number of respects, including the insistent knocking and scratching. The first serious investigator of poltergeists, Allan Kardec, wrote in the 19th century of a case in which such knocking turned out to indicate that a friendly spirit was trying to deliver a message. Once the message had been delivered, he found, the rapping stopped.

"When soldiers are already on parade, the drum is no longer beaten to awaken them," Kardec observed.

An even more typical characteristic of the Durweston case was the apparent involvement of a young child. In this and the Enfield case, as in many other cases, the child was at the age of puberty. The 1981 Winton case also involved children, though not apparently of pubescent age. The members of the Abbott Road household included a seventeen-year-old adopted daughter and an eight-year-old foster son who was also backward. Of these two, it is young Bradley who has attracted most attention. After her visit, Miriam Jeffreys said: "I feel this thing is in Bradley. But he is not being naughty. It is a thing from the devil—a force of light."

In the *Bournemouth Times* on August 22, 1981, David Haith wrote: "Charles is convinced the boy is somehow the innocent focus for the poltergeist energy . . . Throughout the haunting he has rarely shown any emotion. He watches the proceedings quietly with a smile. Witnesses who have seen him closing his eyes, pressing his ears and shaking his head, have wondered if the force is working through him. He also admits to have an 'invisible playmate'."

The article continued: "Alone with Bradley in a wrecked room at his house after one of the poltergeist outbreaks, I found the boy in exuberant mood. He constantly darted about the room picking up toys and broken ornaments and motioning to throw them towards me, all with a mischievous grin. Suddenly, while my back was turned, a tin crashed down from a sideboard, spilling biscuits over the floor. Was it Bradley . . . or the ghost? Almost certainly the boy had toppled the tin but several witnesses have told me they have seen objects move when Bradley was not close by. Could he, like Uri Geller, possess psychic powers to influence matter? There were similar poltergeist outbreaks at the home of now famous psychic Matthew Manning. He later went on to bend spoons, Geller-style, and now has channelled his abilities into new fields. In experiments he has managed to influence cancer cells in test tubes and recently drew huge crowds as a healer and acclaimed worker of miracles. So perhaps Bradley—being tagged the ghost boy by the national media—may after all have a happy future."

Noreen Penfold, the Burdens' clairvoyant natural daughter, who was particularly close to Bradley and looked after him during the two weeks immediately following the Abbott Road happenings, remains convinced that the boy was the unwitting victim of a troubled spirit. She also recalls that he had had a troubled life before joining the family as a foster child.

"We had him from the age of two and when he came he couldn't talk properly," she said. "He used to sit in the corner and make noises like a dog. He was a lovely, lovely kid who just wanted love but was incapable of showing love himself. If he was put to bed at night, he wouldn't sleep but would wander around the house. His eyes were black and when he looked at you he had piercing eyes like in the film *Damion*. He only had to look at a bonfire and it would flare up. He was always talking about his friend Ian, saying that Ian had told him to do so and so, and then laughing."

Mrs. Penfold also recalls that the second seance identified the "troubled spirit" not as the neighbour who had hanged himself but as a member of Debbie's circle of friends, who had died at an early age.

"The spirit was a drug addict who had died and come back through Bradley," she said. "He had shown himself to Bradley as a boy but when all this happened he showed himself as a man. It wasn't very nice at the second seance, apparently. There was a lot of bad language and a lot of cursing because he was a troubled spirit. They found out that his name was Ian and he had known Debbie and had come through Bradley, who was an open channel, an easy channel, because he was retarded. They found out about Ian's addiction and how he died. All he wanted to do was be at peace. Eventually they brought his nan through and they kept saying, 'Do you see the light? Do you see the light?' He said he did and reached out and held his nan's hand. Once through, the voice changed and he said it was beautiful and he was at peace."

Mrs Penfold's interpretation of the Abbott Road events is consistent with one of the leading theories about the nature of poltergeists, namely that ghosts, or spirits of the dead, are able to manifest themselves by somehow absorbing and using energy from their victims. A second theory is that some people, particularly boys and girls at the age of puberty, are able to extrude a force or energy that is capable of intelligent action.

The second seance does seem to have been effective, for the Burden family have never been troubled by poltergeist activity since that time, nor, as far as is known, have any later occupants of 37 Abbott Road. Despite the apparently positive outcome, however, the havoc had

The Burden family's Abbott Road home.

taken its toll on the Burden family, who never were completely reunited. After a few days away from the house, Charles and Kathy felt they could no longer cope with young Bradley and asked that he be taken back into care. They never saw him again. Seven-and-a-half years later, Charles Burden told me: "My wife just couldn't cope any more. Her nerves were smashed and we couldn't look after him. We couldn't blame Bradley for what happened but I believe the spirit picked on him because he was backward. A university professor who came to investigate told me it mostly comes with backward children. It wasn't something Bradley could help. But things only happened when he was around and stopped happening after he had gone. I don't know where he is now. I believe he went to a family in another county and was going to be adopted."

Charles, Kathy, and Deborah returned to 37 Abbott Road after a week, but they also resolved to leave as soon as possible. The house was immediately placed on the market and an application made to Bournemouth Corporation for a council home. This was turned down, but three months later the house was sold for £19,000 to a single man who expressed his intention to renovate it while living there and his conviction that the poltergeist would not return. The Burdens moved to a bungalow at Wallisdown and have since moved to Parkstone. Debbie has moved to the London area, married, and started a family.

10

Who Killed Sandra Court?
The mystery of a motiveless murder, 1986

A few minutes before 3 o'clock on the morning of May 3, 1986, a young woman stepped out of a taxi on the Muscliff housing estate on the outskirts of Bournemouth. She had been driven from Steppes nightclub in St Swithun's Road near the town centre and was intending to spend the rest of the night at her sister's home in Downton Close. She had, as taxi driver Stephen Williams realized, "had a bit to drink". But she was able to get in and out of the cab without any difficulty, was able to talk coherently and was not, in Mr Williams' words, "excessively drunk".

Mr Williams escorted Sandra Court to the door of her sister's house. Her sister was out and Sandra did not have a key but she decided to wait on the doorstep rather than be taken elsewhere, telling the taxi driver that she would get into the house eventually.

They are the last words she is known to have spoken. Almost sixteen hours later, three schoolboys walking three miles away along the Avon Causeway between Hurn village and the Sopley-to-Ringwood road noticed the body of a woman lying in a water-filled ditch. It was later identified as that of Sandra Court and a post-mortem examination revealed that she had been strangled. Detectives concluded that she had probably been taken out of a car nearby, carried across the bank, and then either placed in the water or thrown over the railings into the ditch. But the exact circumstances of her death and the identity of her killer were destined to remain a mystery even after a long and intensive police investigation, a blaze of publicity, and a full inquest by a coroner and jury.

Sandra Court was twenty-seven at the time of her death. She was a girl who loved life and lived it to the full. She was also immensely popular, with friends in abundance and no known enemies. Those who knew her remember her as lively and humorous. She also had an

Sandra Court.

independent streak to the point of being headstrong.

"She was," her mother, Beryl Court, told me in an interview for the *Bournemouth Evening Echo* soon after Sandra's death, "an adventuress. She went on a parachuting course, she was a qualified lifeguard and every Boxing Day she went on an all-night hike with the Venture Scouts."

Sandra was the eldest of Bill and Beryl Court's three childen—two girls and a boy—and was brought up in a loving, stable, and close-knit family. As a girl, she went to Winton Infants and Junior schools in Bournemouth and Glenmoor School for Girls. She was also in the Brownies, Guides, Sea Rangers, and Venture Scouts and was a Queen's Guide. For a time she belonged to the Southern Skirmishers, who re-enact battles from the American Civil War.

After leaving school at sixteen, Sandra went to college at the Lansdowne before working in a car taxation office, as an auxiliary nurse at Poole General Hospital, and finally as an administrative clerk with the Bournemouth-based life assurance company Abbey Life and its subsidiary, Ambassador Life. The day before her death was also her last day of employment with Ambassador, for she was planning to start a new life as a children's nanny on the Mediterranean island of Majorca the following week.

Sandra's last day at work was taken up largely with farewell celebrations, which began with a pizza lunch with forty colleagues and continued in the evening with a party at the Abbey Life social club. Her sister, Jenny, recalls that when she arrived at the social club, Sandra was already "giggly, merry and quite drunk".

"She was," Jenny told an inquest months later, "drinking white wine and soda and having a good time, though she cried because she was sorry to be leaving."

Jenny last saw her sister alive at 10.30 p.m. on May 2, at which time she was "fairly drunk" and expressed her intention to go to Steppes nightclub, where she had been the previous night. Jenny thought Sandra had already had enough to drink and tried to persuade her to come home instead but her sister replied: "I'm twenty-seven and can do what I like."

"I was concerned," Jenny told the inquest. "I told my boyfriend and he went to look for her in Holdenhurst Road, but she had gone."

A colleague of Sandra, John Hewlett, who saw her in Holdenhurst Road as she headed for Steppes, said she was zigzagging and he took her by the arm to lead her across the road. She asked him to go to the club with her but he declined. She told him she wanted to see a girl there called Angie, whom she got on well with and who had not been to the farewell celebration.

When police began their murder investigation following the discovery of Sandra's body the following evening, they were immediately struck by the apparent absence of motive. A narrow ligature had been used to strangle her but it was clear than only minimal force had been applied and there was nothing to indicate that there had been a struggle. She was fully clothed apart from her shoes

Police led by Detective Chief Superintendent Alan Rose search the Avon Causeway ditch for clues. *(Photo: Bob Richardson, Evening Echo, Bournemouth)*

and there was no evidence of sexual interference. And although her shoes, woollen jacket, handbag, and certain items of jewellery were missing, nothing of great value was involved, nor was any large sum of money.

Alan Rose, who led the inquiry as head of Dorset CID before his subsequent promotion to Assistant Chief Constable, said at the time: "It is a puzzling and unusual case which does not fit any of the usual patterns. She may have been killed for the £20 in her purse but there is no obvious motive at all and we are keeping an open mind."

Twenty-four hours passed before the police became aware of the dead woman's identity. Her parents were unaware of the discovery and had assumed that their daughter was staying with friends. They began to worry only when she failed to arrive for lunch on the Sunday. Later that day, a friend of the family contacted the police and their worst fears were confirmed. It was their second tragedy in two days, for on the day before Sandra's death, her "adopted" aunt had died suddenly of a brain haemorrhage at the age of fifty-three.

Strangulation was soon established as the cause of Sandra's death, but Home Office pathologist Dr Bill Kennard concluded that little force had been used. He reported that the ligature mark was one-and-a-quarter inches wide and seven inches long, was not caused by hands but by a "thin scarf or something similar". He also concluded that Sandra was dead before her body was dumped in the ditch and that she had died at least twelve hours before her body was found at 6.45 p.m. on May 3.

The murder investigation was to become one of the biggest and most intensive ever mounted by Dorset police, costing £500,000 and involving a team of more than 100 detectives for several months of 1986 and a smaller team for a much longer period. The team included Woman Detective Sergeant Angie Smith, who was assigned to play a vital role, spending several hours a day with the Court family, partly to help them with any problems that might arise, but also to build up as comprehensive a picture as possible of the murdered girl.

Among the priorities in the early days of the investigation were the reconstruction of Sandra's movements during the last hours of her life and the recovery of her missing belongings. As inquiries got under way and the public became aware of the case through widespread media coverage, the first witnesses began to come forward. These included a cyclist, who had found Sandra's gold and pearl necklace on a verge about half-a-mile from the spot where her body was discovered, and a handful of people who believed they had seen her in Bournemouth during the early hours of May 3.

It was soon established that Sandra remained at the Steppes nightclub from about 10.45 p.m. until she boarded Mr Williams' taxi at 2.45 the following morning and that he had left her outside the house in Downton Close a few minutes later. It also became clear that, having failed to get into the house, she must have set off on foot within a fairly short time after Mr Williams' departure. At 3.15, a girl answering her description was seen by a milkman at the Unigate depot in Belmont Avenue, off Castle Lane, and at 3.45 two teenage girls walking home from a party saw someone who may have been Sandra near the junction of Castle Lane and Wimborne Road. They said that she was walking slowly and swaying as she did so and was carrying her shoes in her hand. They concluded that she was drunk. Another possible sighting just before 5 a.m., near Charminster Library, suggested that Sandra may then have been heading for Five Ways at Charminster. Her family and detectives were puzzled by the sightings, which implied that she was not heading for her parents' home in Forest View Road, Moordown, as they would have expected her to do.

The first of Sandra's missing possessions to be handed to the police was the gold and pearl necklace given to her by colleagues as a leaving present on the day before she died. It was found by a cyclist near the

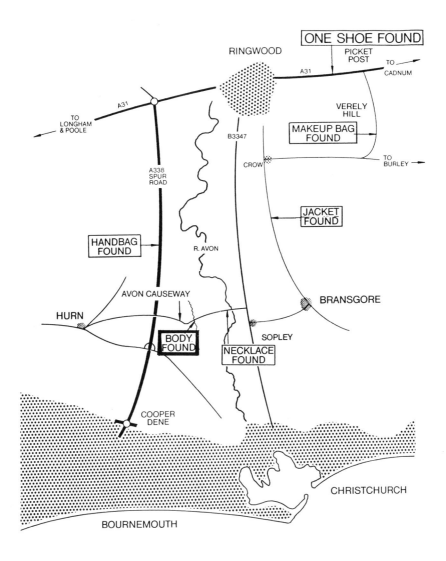

A police map of the area where Sandra Court's body and belongings were found.

bridge over the River Avon in Avon Causeway on May 3 but the police were not notified until May 6. On this or the following day, another member of the public saw Sandra's cerise-coloured woollen jacket in a stream alongside Crow Lane, near Bransgore, and this was given to detectives on May 9.

Other finds followed. Her handbag was found on May 8 beside the southbound carriageway of the Ringwood-to-Bournemouth spur road, her cosmetic bag on May 11 at the Verely Hill car park in the New Forest, and half of her Barclaycard and part of her Phonecard on May 12 beside the eastbound carriageway of the A31 trunk road near Stoney Cross. All these finds were made by members of the public, but on May 12 the police themselves discovered Sandra's left shoe on a ditch beside the A31 westbound carriageway near the turning to Poulner Hill Farm, near Ringwood.

There were no more finds of significance until May 27, when a renewed police search yielded seven separate discoveries involving parts of Sandra Court's Barclaycard and Phonecard and torn fragments of her Midland Bank cheque book in the Picket Post area of the A31.

The killer or killers appeared to have driven many miles in East Dorset and the New Forest, taking a roughly circular route and scattering Sandra Court's belongings as they did so. By a tragic irony, most of the area involved was overlooked by Bill and Beryl Court's home in Moordown, which commands a panoramic view of the Avon Valley. Detectives were uncertain about the motive of the killer or killers in scattering the items so widely. As Detective Chief Superintendent Rose said: "We don't know whether the killer was being devious or simply panicking."

In the meantime, the police had also discovered that they were not the only ones trying to track down the killer. The intriguing nature of the clues, plus the prospect of a £10,000 reward (offered anonymously as the inquiry entered its second week), was turning the case into a real-life game of Cluedo. An army of armchair detectives was emerging Miss Marple-like from the suburbs of Bournemouth and district to add their theories and suggestions to the accumulation of evidence.

"They are following the trail of clues as details appear in the press, then ringing the incident room at Boscombe to put forward their interpretations," said the then deputy head of Dorset CID, Des Donohoe, on May 20. "We have received literally dozens of separate theories. Each one is examined to see if it has any merit. It's pleasing to see the efforts people are making to help us try and catch this murderer."

During the first twelve days of the inquiry, police received more

DORSET POLICE

MURDER OF
SANDRA JILL COURT

Between 3 a.m. and 7 p.m.
SATURDAY 3rd MAY 1986

REWARD
£10,000

FOR INFORMATION LEADING TO
THE ARREST AND CONVICTION OF
THE OFFENDER(S)

If you have any information please contact
the Incident Room on
BOURNEMOUTH (0202) 22099
or any Police Station

B. Weight
Chief Constable

The reward poster.

than eight hundred calls from members of the public. They also filed 10,000 cross-referenced index cards and labelled 330 separate exhibits relating to the case, ranging from a hair to a bicycle. Everyone known to have been closely connected with Sandra in the recent past was interviewed, including former boyfriends and her ex-fiancé (she had been engaged a couple of years before), colleagues from the Abbey Life group, and people whom she met at Steppes nightclub a few hours before her death. Steppes was known in Bournemouth as a "gay" club, but police found nothing to convince them that Sandra Court had a lesbian background. Her association with the club and some of its members was as brief as it was recent.

Police were also keen to trace three motorists whose vehicles were seen in the Hurn area in the early hours of May 3. One vehicle, parked beside the spur road near Blackwater Bridge at 3.20 a.m. with its hazard lights flashing, was occupied by a man and a woman, who spoke to another motorist who stopped to ask if they were all right. A second car—a red Ford XR3—pulled into a gateway near Hurn Airport runway in Matchams Lane at about 4 a.m. but was later eliminated from the inquiry after the driver voluntarily responded to a police appeal. The third vehicle is believed to have driven along the Avon Causeway at 5.20 a.m. on May 3.

At one stage in the investigation, detectives even flew to Spain to interview an Englishman who lived there but had been in Bournemouth around the time of Sandra's death. He, too, was ruled out as a suspect.

But the most dramatic development was yet to come. On the afternoon of Tuesday May 20, Detective Chief Superintendent Rose opened a letter that he believed had been written by someone close to Sandra's killer. It was correctly addressed to him personally, bore a second-class stamp, and carried the Southampton postmark and the date of May 16. The letter, which was almost but not entirely devoid of punctuation, read:

"dear Sir I am writing to tell you that the tragic death of Sandra Court was a complete and utter accident, in no form is the person a killer or murderer the person concerned is deeply unhappy, hurt, and in total shock the only reason the person has not come forward is the fact of being afraid that their explanation will not be believed Please I beg take this letter to be of the truth"

It appeared that the writer of the letter had disguised his or her writing and experts confirmed this. Mr Rose delayed making the exact contents of the letter public for several days and instead asked the *Evening Echo* to publish a personal appeal, which he hoped would be

Dear Sir I am writing to tell you that the tragic death of Sandra Court was a complete and utter accident, in no form is the person a killer or murderer the person concerned is deeply unhappy, hurt, and in total shock the only reason the person has not come forward is the fact of being afraid that their explanation will not be believed Please I beg take this letter to be of the truth

The anonymous letter, posted in the Southampton area, thought to be from someone close to the killer.

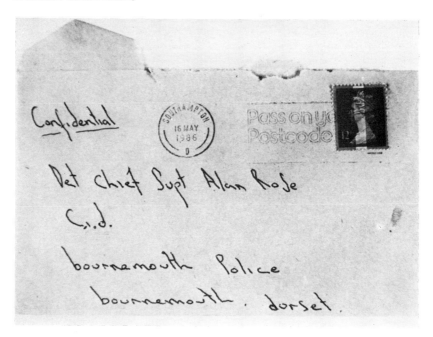

read by the writer. As the paper's chief reporter at the time, I was assigned to write the story. Mr Rose told me that he believed the letter to be genuine: "My feeling when I read it was that it was most certainly written by someone close to the person responsible for Sandy's death," he said. "We think it's possibly from the offender's nearest and dearest—a mother, perhaps, or a wife—someone who obviously knows what the offender has done. The explanation which the letter puts forward for Sandy's death is feasible and is something we have already considered and, if it is correct, then the person responsible owes it to himself or herself to come forward."

But the person did not come forward, either at that time or when, a few days later, Mr Rose released photographs of the letter and its envelope to the media. As the weeks went by, the flow of useful information into the murder squad headquarters began to decline. The weeks turned into months and, as they did so, hopes that the case would be brought to a swift and satisfactory conclusion began to recede. Eventually, the police operation was scaled down, permission was given for Sandra's family to go ahead with the funeral, and an

146

inquest was arranged. By this time, the police had devoted 61,782 man hours to the inquiry, taken almost 5,000 sets of fingerprints, and recorded 4,300 statements from 3,686 people.

Several senior detectives attended the funeral at Bournemouth Crematorium on January 30, 1987, partly as a tribute to the girl they had never known but about whom they now knew so much, partly to scan the mourners for any clues that might lead them to Sandra's killer. Nearly two hundred people attended the service, crowding into the aisles and adjoining chapel once the eighty seats had all been taken. The procession filed in to the gentle organ accompaniment of "Morning Has Broken", one of Sandra's favourite hymns. "The Lord is my Shepherd" was also sung, at the request of her parents.

The Rev. Raymond Short, Minister of the Punshon Methodist Church in Bournemouth, who conducted the service, described Sandra as a "lively, friendly and adventurous person", with a "zest and determination" about life and also a "great characater who enriched the lives of those who knew her". Mr Short also spoke of the mysteries of life and death and added: "For Sandra, there is the added mystery of why and how she died."

The inquest was held at Poole Magistrates' Court and began on February 25, 1987, before a jury of five men and five women. The East Dorset Coroner, Mr Nigel Neville-Jones, outlined the circumstances of Sandra's death and the events leading up to it and read the anonymous letter sent to Mr Rose.

"The police do receive letters written for scurrilous reasons but here we have a letter which, when one looks at it, may indeed contain the truth," he said. "Forensic tests have been carried out on it, as a result of which it has become known that the handwriting was heavily disguised and because of that, the writer could not be identified. It may well have been written by a person who knows the identity of the person or persons responsible for Miss Court's death. Great force was not used, so there is a possibility that it was an accident. But that doesn't mean the person was not responsible for her death. Clearly someone knows and that person must be found."

Evidence was called from witnesses who knew Sandra or saw her during the last hours of her life, from the Home Office pathologist, and from detectives involved in the case. It was also called from a middle-aged Bournemouth man called Brian Pacifico, who had been interrogated at length by police several months before after finding items belonging to Sandra Court in two different places nine days apart. Mr Pacifico told the inquest that he was the person who found Sandra's necklace beside the road in Avon Causeway on May 3. He

147

said he put it in his pocket and gave it to a twelve-year-old girl from the Boscombe congregation of Jehovah's Witness with which he was associated. Several days later, after hearing that the police were looking for a necklace, he told them about the find and took them to the girl's house.

Mr Pacifico said that it was during another cycle ride on May 12 that, while pushing his cycle up an incline on the A31 between Picket Post and Stoney Cross, he noticed half a Barclaycard on the verge.

"It was in fairly new, gleaming condition and I saw the name S. J. Court," he said, adding that he immediately reported the discovery and was soon afterwards arrested, cautioned, and interviewed.

The Coroner asked Mr Pacifico: "Have you any connection whatsoever with the death of Sandra Court?"

"No, sir," he replied.

Later, Mr Neville-Jones observed: "I'm sure you will agree that it was a coincidence that you found these items."

Mr Pacifico: "Not such a tremendous coincidence because I was following what was the straight line from Castle Lane to the body to the necklace to the jacket to the bag."

He added that he was "riding for pleasure", but agreed that he had given "careful thought" to the route the killer might have taken and had thought it likely that he might find something on that route. He denied that he was a bounty hunter or a "self-appointed Sherlock Holmes or Maigret" but when asked by the Coroner if he was "a bit of a magpie", he answered: "Yes, very much so."

Mr Pacifico spent about one-and-a-half hours in the witness box during the second day of the inquest and was questioned at length by the Coroner, a police representative, and members of the jury. At the end of the questioning, the jury requested an adjournment on the grounds that they wished to hear from two people mentioned by Mr Pacifico in his evidence. One was a friend at Southampton, whom he said he was intending to visit on the day he made his find beside the A31 at Picket Post; the other was a Bournemouth acquaintance who had told Mr Pacifico that he had seen Sandra Court and two other girls in Wimborne Road in the early hours of May 3. In response to this, Detective Superintendent Richard Thomas of Dorset CID told the inquest that he thought the latter person had already been interviewed by the police, and this would be checked, but he thought it was the first they had heard of Mr Pacifico's friend at Southampton.

Mr Neville-Jones granted a five-day adjournment, telling the jury: "I think you have made a wise decision."

When the hearing was resumed on March 3, however, the

Brian Pacifico, who found discarded belongings of Sandra Court, leaves the inquest at Poole. *(Photo: Richard Crease, Evening Echo, Bournemouth)*

149

outstanding matters were dealt with in a few minutes, the Coroner reading statements signed by the two people to whom Mr Pacifico had referred. One of them confirmed that Mr Pacifico was a keen cyclist who rode great distances and who often "picks up pieces of paper and odd things at the roadside". After a twenty-five-minute summing up, Mr Neville-Jones invited the jury to consider three possible verdicts— unlawful killing, accidental death, and an open verdict. It took the jurors less than ten minutes to reach their unanimous conclusion that Sandra Court was unlawfully killed. The Coroner commented: "The police investigation will continue and I certainly hope that the person or persons responsible for Miss Court's death will be apprehended."

Three years after the killing, the case remained unsolved and detectives and the Court family were still unaware of exactly how, when, and where Sandra met her death and who was responsible for it. It is the mystery that, for her parents, is the greatest cause of anguish. As her mother told me on the first anniversary of Sandra's death: "You keep imagining all sorts of things. You wonder whether she suffered and if so, how she suffered. For all we know, she could have known that something terrible was going to happen."

Referring to the four-hour time lapse between the last sighting of Sandra and the latest possible time of her death, Mrs Court added: "She could have been driven round in a terrified state for hours."

Both the family and the police continue to give credence to the anonymous letter claiming that Sandra's death was an accident. As recently as the early weeks of 1989, a telephone call, also anonymous, was made to the BBC television programme "Crimewatch UK" referring to the letter and reiterating the claim.

"I am in no doubt," says Detective Chief Superintendent Des Donohoe, who has since become head of Dorset CID, "that there is somebody in this county or a neighbouring county who knows something about the death of Sandra Court, and my greatest disappointment is that we did not get that person to come forward and do what is right by any rule of society. I am also aware that sometimes people do find themselves in circumstances that go horribly wrong and I have an understanding of how these things can happen. It need not necessarily be the end of the world. I do believe that confession is good for the soul and I believe there is someone out there who is still going through torment. My hope is that that person may yet decide to come forward."

The possibility that such a person may come forward is one remaining strand of hope for those who, even now, seek to establish who killed Sandra Court and how they came to do so. A second strand of hope is that the police do have in their possession one small piece of evidence, which they believe could one day identify the killer. It is a fingerprint found on a torn piece of Sandra Court's cheque book recovered from the roadside on the A31 trunk route. Everyone who could have handled the cheque book, including printers and bank officials, has been fingerprinted and eliminated from the inquiry and police believe the print can belong only to the person who tore up the cheque book.

"If we match the fingerprint, we find the murderer," said Detective Chief Superintendent Donohoe.

SOURCES

Murder in the High Street

Poole Museums Service, *Three Museums in Poole*
Smith, H. P., *Official Guide to the Old Town House* (1929)
Smith, H. P. *The History of the Borough and County of the Town of Poole* (1948)
Underwood, Peter, *Ghosts of Dorset* (1988)
Wilnecker, Pat, *The High Street Murders 1598* (1980)

The Ghost in the Gallery
"A true account and narrative of an apparition in the County of Dorset" (Dorset Record Office D/WLC/Z22)
Beaminster manorial presentments (Dorset Record Office 6272)
Beaminster parish registers, copies of Bishop's transcripts, and other parish documents (Dorset Record Office)
Eedle, Marie de G., *A History of Beaminster* (1984)
Eedle, Marie de G., and Paul, E. Raymond, *The Death and Times of John Daniel* (1987)
Gentleman's Magazine (1774)
Hine, Richard, *History of Beaminster* (1914)
Hole, Christina, *Haunted England: A Survey of English Ghost-lore (1940)*
Hutchins, John, and continuators, *The History and Antiquities of the County of Dorset,* vol. II (3rd edition, 1861-70)
Notice of coroner's inquest into John Daniel's death (Dorset Record Office D131/X8)

The Gypsies' Alibi
Darton, F. J. Harvey, *Alibi Pilgrimage* (1936)
Darton, F. J. Harvey, *The Marches of Wessex* (1922, 1936)
Torre, Lilian de la, *Elizabeth is Missing* (1947)

The Coffin in the Crypt

Fane, F., "A Legend of Milton" *(Proceedings of the Dorset Natural History and Antiquarian Field Club,* vol. XVI, 1895)

Inquest papers into the death of John Damer (1776, Westminster Abbey Muniment Room and Library)

Milton Abbas parish registers (Dorset Record Office)

Noble, Percy, *Anne Seymour Damer: A Woman of Art and Fashion 1748-1828* (1908)

Traskey, J. P., *Milton Abbey: A Dorset Monastery in the Middle Ages* (1978)

Wansbrough, Richard, *The Tale of Milton Abbas* (1974)

Western Flying Post or Sherborne and Yeovil Mercury (1776)

White, Maria L., *Westminster Inquests* (1980, unpublished, Westminster Abbey Muniment Room and Library)

The Tarrant Valley Vampire

Cecil, David, *Some Dorset Country Houses: a personal selection* (1985)

Darton, F. J. Harvey, *The Marches of Wessex* (1922, 1936)

Dorset marriage index of the Somerset and Dorset Family History Society

Hawkins, Desmond, *Cranborne Chase* (1981)

Hole, Christina, *Haunted England: A Survey of English Ghost-lore (1940)*

Hutchins, John, and continuators, *The History and Antiquities of the County of Dorset,* 3 editions (1774–1870)

Legg, Rodney, Collier, Mary, and Perrott, Tom, *Ghosts of Dorset, Devon and Somerset* (1974)

Legg, Rodney, *Mysterious Dorset* (1987)

Parish registers of Tarrant Gunville and Winterborne Houghton (Dorset County Record Office)

Recollections of Peter Farquharson

Sale, Richard, and Ang, Tom *Dorset* (1985)

Tarrant Gunville vestry minute book

The Witch and the Parson

Bettey, J. H., *Rural Life in Wessex 1500-1900* (1977)

Brocklebank, Joan, *Affpuddle in the County of Dorset AD 987-1953* (1968)

Darton, F. J. Harvey, *The Marches of Wessex* (1922, 1936)

Davies, G. J. (ed.), *Touchyng Witchcrafte and Sorcerye* (1985)

Hole, Christina (ed)., *Witchcraft at Toner's Puddle, 19th C: From the diary of the Rev. William Ettrick* (1964)

Hutchins, John, and continuators, *The History and Antiquities of the County of Dorset,* vol. I (3rd edition, 1861-70)

Legg, Rodney, *Mysterious Dorset* (1987)

Lloyd, Polly, *Legends of Dorset* (1988)

Philpott, Olive M., "The Puddle Valley" (*Dorset Year Book, 1946-7)*

Richardson, John, *The Local Historian's Encyclopedia* (1986)
Street, Sean, *Tales of Old Dorset* (1985)
Turnerspuddle parish registers (Dorset Record Office)
Weinstock, M. B., *Old Dorset* (1967)

The Grave of the Ripper?
Cullen, Tom, *Autumn of Terror: Jack the Ripper, His Crimes and Times* (1965)
Dorset County Chronicle and Somersetshire Gazette (1889)
Farson, Daniel, *Jack the Ripper* (1972)
Honeycombe, Gordon, *The Murders of the Black Museum 1870-1970* (1982)
Howells, Martin and Skinner, Keith, *The Ripper Legacy (1987)*
Knight, Stephen, *Jack the Ripper: the Final Solution* (1977)
Rumbelow, Donald, *The Complete Jack the Ripper* (1987)
Wilson, Colin and Odell, Robin, *Jack the Ripper: Summing Up and Verdict* (1987)

The Car at Cloud's Hill
Bournemouth Evening Echo, Dorset County Chronicle, Dorset Evening Echo, Dorset the County Magazine, Western Gazette
Legg, Rodney, *Lawrence of Arabia in Dorset* (1988)
Mack, John E., *A Prince of Disorder* (1976)
Miller, Alan J., *Stories from Dorset History (1987)*
Stewart, Desmond, *T. E. Lawrence* (1977)
Yardley, Michael, *Backing into the Limelight* (1985)

The Winton Wrecker
Bournemouth Evening Echo, Bournemouth Times, Daily Mirror, Daily Star
Bord, Janet and Colin, *Modern Mysteries of Britain: One hundred years of strange events*
Cavendish, Richard (editor), *Encyclopaedia of the Unexplained* (1974)
Legg, Rodney, *Mysterious Dorset* (1987)
Playfair, Guy Lyon, *This House is Haunted: An investigation of the Enfield Poltergeist* (1980)
Recollections of Charles Burden, Noreen Penfold, and officers of the Dorset police (communicated orally to the author)

Who Killed Sandra Court?
Bournemouth Evening Echo
Notes and recollections of the author relating to his own involvement in coverage of the Sandra Court murder inquiry for the *Evening Echo,* in particular interviews with senior detectives and the Court family and personal attendance of the funeral and inquest.

ACKNOWLEDGEMENTS

I am grateful to everyone who has assisted either directly or indirectly in the production of this book, in particular to Bob Richardson, Duncan Lee, Julie Bull, Arthur Grant, David Graves, and Paul Williams for photographic work; to Pat Fleming, editor of the *Evening Echo*, Bournemouth, for their permission to use pictures and text; and to the following for their co-operation in providing information: Chris Adamson, Charles Burden, Noreen Penfold, Peter Farquharson, the Rev. David Stevens, Harold Paish, Mary Coalbran, Daphne Hills, the staff of the Dorset County Record Office, the Dorset County Library, and the Westminster Abbey muniment-room and, from the Dorset Constabulary, Assistant Chief Constable Alan Rose, head of CID Detective Chief Superintendent Des Donohoe, Superintendent Peter Williams, and PC Graham Joyce.

I must also acknowledge the many other researchers and writers without whose work, published and unpublished, a book of this kind is impossible, especially Pat Wilnecker, whom I have never met but on whose booklet on the Poole High Street murders I have drawn heavily.

Finally, I would like to offer a special word of thanks, and also of admiration, to Bill and Beryl Court, whom I came to know quite well as a result of the tragedy that befell them in 1986. The extent of their tolerance and co-operation in such circumstances continues to amaze me and I hope they will see the final chapter as the tribute to their daughter that, in a way, it is.

INDEX